CORPORATE TAXATION IN THE DUTCH CARIBBEAN AND LATIN AMERICAN REGION

CORPORATE TAXATION IN THE DUTCH CARIBBEAN AND LATIN AMERICAN REGION

Aruba, BES Islands, Brazil, Colombia, Curaçao, Mexico, Peru and Venezuela

Prof. Dr. Anouk Bollen-Vandenboorn
(coordinator)

ISBN: 9789082960105

The content and opinions expressed in this publication are solely those of the author(s).

Buenos Aires

TeseoPress Design (www.teseopress.com)

Table of Contents

Foreword

In this book the authors provide a glimpse of the corporate tax systems of certain Latin American countries, establishing how these systems work in domestic and in cross-border situations. In that sense, even though these countries are mainly importers of foreign investments, attention is also paid to the treatment granted to income earned by resident corporations abroad.

The first chapter of the book focuses on the relations between Curaçao and Sint Maarten with The Netherlands, while the following chapters are dedicated to the tax systems of Aruba and Curaçao, Brazil, Colombia, Mexico, Peru and Venezuela. To facilitate a comparative study of the tax treatment of resident and non-resident corporations in these countries, the chapters are structured in a similar manner.

The analysis of the corporate tax systems of the states starts on the study of the tax treatment of corporations at domestic level. Only after this situation is carefully presented the authors move on to analyze the corporate income tax at international level. The study is further complemented by the analysis, respectively, of eventual anti-avoidance legislation, tax treaty law, community law, influence of BEPS Action Plan on the tax system of the countries and, finally, attention is paid to jurisprudence regarding the corporate income tax system.

The study of the chapters shows that despite the differences between the countries, there are similarities in the structuring of their corporate tax systems, which means that, despite the lack of a monetary/customs union between these states, further cooperation could be beneficial for the development of a uniform approach regarding the taxation of corporate profits earned by non-resident enterprises and on how to tackle abusive situations. The chapters of this book, which were first drafted in 2016 under the edition of Dr. Esperanza Buitrago, who paved the way to make this book a reality, are updated up to July 2017.

Dr. Fernando Souza de Man
Editor

Words of Gratitude & Appreciation

We would like to thank all authors and the editor for all the work and their commitment to this book.

The first DDMP book!

September 2016 was the start of the Double Degree Master Program (DDMP) in International and European Tax Law, American Specialization. This program, a joint venture between Maastricht University (Europe) and the University of Aruba, aims to deliver high qualified tax lawyers for the Latin American countries and the Caribbean. This means that the excellent courses in this program have a special focus on this area in combination with the standards and developments in the US and Europe.

This book is part of the DDMP, more specific the Course on Comparative Dutch Caribbean and Latin American Tax Law. We are very grateful to all people who make this book possible.

We express our highest appreciation to:

- Prof. Dr. Roland Brandsma
- Juan Rafael Bravo Gaviria, LL.M
- Esperanza Buitrago Diaz Ph.D
- Fernando Nuñez, LL.M
- Ana Paula Pardo Lelo de Larrea, LL.M
- Winston Perez, LL.M
- Hans Ruiter, LL.M
- Jorge San Martín, CPA, J.D
- Fernando Souza de Man, Ph.D
- Sandy van Thol, LL.M

Yours sincerely,

Prof. Dr. Anouk Bollen-Vandenboorn

Maastricht University
Director of the Double Degree Program
in International and European Tax Law,
American Specialisation
www.maastrichtuniversity.nl/law/aruba

List of Authors

Prof. Dr. Roland Brandsma

Professor of Fiscal Economics at the University of Amsterdam and Professor of General Tax Law at Nyenrode Business University. Substitute Judge of the Court of Appeal of The Hague. Tax Partner at PwC Netherlands. Master in Tax Law, Leiden University. Master in Civil Law, University of Amsterdam. Master in Cultural Anthropology, Leiden University. PhD in Tax Law, Leiden University.

Juan Rafael Bravo Gaviria, LL.M

Senior Associate at Bravo Abogados. Professor of International Tax Law in the Postgraduate Specialization in Tax Law from Rosario University. Bachelor of Law and Bachelor of Economics, Rosario University. LL.M in International and European Tax Law, Maastricht University. Member of The Colombian Tax Institute.

Dr. Esperanza Buitrago Diaz

Director of the Postgraduate Course on International and European Tax Law Course of the Maastricht Center for Taxation at Campus Brussel, where she is also part of the teaching staff. Academic at the service of the *Maastricht Center for Taxation (MCT) at Maastricht University.* Professor of International Tax Law at Master program at the Universidad Externado de Colombia. Bachelor of Law, Universidad de La Sabana, Master Financial Law, Rosario University and Master Intellectual Property, Universidad de los Andes. PhD (*summa cum laude*), University of Salamanca. Member of Research Tax Law Centre of Colombian Tax Institute and alumni of the Max Planck Institute for Tax Law and Public Finance, Germany. Winner of prize on International Taxation granted by the University of Valencia and Deloitte in 2007 and of the Extraordinary Prize of Salamanca University in 2007.

Fernando Nuñez, LL.M

Tax Partner at Estudio Hernandez & Cia. Abogados. Professor of LL.M Tax programs at Universidad de Lima and Universidad ESAN. Bachelor of Law, Universidade de Lima. LL.M in International and European Tax Law, Maastricht University. Member of the International Fiscal Association (IFA) and the Society of Trust and Estate Practicioners (STEP).

Ana Paula Pardo Lelo de Larrea, LL.M

Tax Partner at SMPS Legal. Bachelor of Law, Universidad Panamericana. LL.M in International Taxation, University of Florida – Fredric G. Levin College of Law. Member of IBA (International Bar Association), IFA (International Fiscal Association).

Winston Perez, LL.M

Tax advisor at Grant Thornton Curaçao. Previously at PwC Venezuela, Deloitte Venezuela, PwC Dutch Caribbean. Bachelor of Law, Universidad Santa Maria. Master in Taxation, Universidad Metropolitana. Lecturer at the Comparative Dutch Caribbean and Latin American Tax Law at the Double Degree Programme on International and European Tax Law, American Specialization, Aruba University and Maastricht.

Hans Ruiter, LL.M

Tax Partner at Grant Thornton, Dutch Caribbean. Former Partner of PwC Aruba. Professor of Comparative Dutch Caribbean and Latin American Tax Law at the Double Degree Programme on International and European Tax Law, American Specialization, Aruba University and Maastricht University. Founder and board member of the Aruban Association of Tax Advisors. Master in Tax Law, University of Amsterdam.

Jorge San Martín, CPA, J.D.

Tax partner at SMPS Legal. Former tax partner at Gardere Wynne Sewell LLP (Mexico office) and Accountancy firm Rocha, Pérez, San Martín, S.C. Bachelor of Law, Universidad Nacional Autónoma México and Bachelor of Accountancy, Universidad Anáhuac del Norte. Member of the Mexican Public Accountant's School and Mexican Institute of Public Accountants. Member of the American Chamber of Commerce and Canadian Member of Commerce, Mexico City.

Dr. Fernando Souza de Man

Assistant Professor at Maastricht University. Bachelor of Law, University of Sao Paulo. LL.M in International and European Tax Law, Maastricht University. PhD, Maastricht University. Member of the Scientific Committee of the Brazilian Institute of Tax Law.

Sandy van Thol, LL.M

Founder and Managing Director of Sotto Voce Business & Tax Solutions. Lecturer at the Comparative Dutch Caribbean and Latin American Tax Law at the Double Degree Programme on International and European Tax Law, American Specialization, Aruba University and Maastricht. Bachelor of Law, Maastricht University. LL.M, Maastricht University.

1

Tax Agreement between the Netherlands and Curaçao and the Tax Agreement between the Netherlands and St. Maarten[1]

PROF. DR. ROLAND P.C.W.M. BRANDSMA[2]

On 10 October 2010 (10/10/10), the constitutional structure changed significantly within the Kingdom of the Netherlands. Previously the Kingdom of the Netherlands consisted of three countries, namely Aruba, the Netherlands Antilles and the Netherlands. The fiscal relations between these three countries were (and partly still are) regulated by the Tax Regulations for the Kingdom (TRK).

The Kingdom of the Netherlands consists of four countries after the constitutional amendments, namely Aruba, Curaçao, St. Maarten and the Netherlands and three special municipalities, namely Bonaire, St. Eustatius and Saba. A separate arrangement was established between the latter municipalities, that have their own fiscal regime,

---

[1] This article is an actualized and more comprehensive version of a published article co-authored with A. Kattouw and S.R. Vanenburg. The initial article, written in Dutch, has been published in the Weekblad voor Fiscaal Recht 2014, p. 1437 and further. Mr. A. Kattouw and Mr. S.R. Vanenburg work for PwC Curacao.
[2] Professor Roland P.C.W.M. Brandsma works for PwC Nederland. In addition, Prof. Roland P.C.W.M. Brandsma works for the University of Amsterdam and Nyenrode Business University.

and the European part of the Netherlands. This separate arrangement was mentioned as the Tax Regulation Netherlands.

Initially the fiscal relations between the countries of the Kingdom of the Netherlands were regulated by the TRK. However, it soon became clear that the intention was to replace the TRK by bilateral tax agreements.

As of 1 December 2015, the Bilateral Tax Agreement Netherlands Curaçao (TANC) has replaced the old TRK. Under the new agreement the taxation rights between both countries have been more aligned with the OECD Model Convention (OECD MC) compared to the TRK. Under the new agreement it is possible, under specific conditions, to reduce the Dutch dividend withholding tax rate on dividend distributions to Curaçao to 0%. In addition, the period in which the Netherlands has the taxation rights is extended in case of a substantial interest, pensions and inheritances or donations. The TANC includes a specific regulation for hybrid entities where the source country follows the (whether or not) hybrid qualification of that entity in another country. The TANC applies to fiscal years and fiscal periods starting on or after 1 January 2016. In case of taxes withheld at source, the new agreement is applicable to payments made on or after 1 January 2016.

As of 1 March 2016, the Tax Agreement Netherlands-St. Maarten (TANSM) has come into effect. This agreement differs only on a few points from the TANC. The TANSM will be discussed briefly in section 10. No new tax agreements have been concluded between the Netherlands and Aruba and between the Caribbean islands themselves. As a result, the TRK remains fully applicable in these situations.

I. Introduction

The proposal for the new tax agreement, that gives form to the fiscal relations between the Netherlands and Curaçao, was published on 10 June 2014.[3] This agreement replaces the Tax Regulation for the Kingdom (TRK).

II. Background

The TRK was established in 1965 when the Kingdom of the Netherlands consisted of the Netherlands, Suriname and the Netherlands Antilles. As a result of the constitutional amendments, particularly the independence of Suriname in 1975, Aruba's withdrawal from the Netherlands Antilles in 1986 and the dissolution of the Netherlands Antilles in 2010, five different tax systems are currently applicable in four countries[4]. Consequently, the TRK was no longer readily applicable in the new relationships. Therefore, it has been decided to replace the TRK by bilateral tax agreements, at least between the Netherlands and other countries within the Kingdom of the Netherlands.[5] Bilateral tax agreements provide the advantage that going forward no complete agreement needs to be reached between all countries of the Kingdom of the Netherlands.

Moreover, bilateral tax agreements make room for the individual position of the various countries. For example, Aruba and Curaçao have a larger financial sector than St. Maarten. Therefore, the interests of Aruba and Curaçao

---

3   Parliamentary Papers II 2013/14, 33 955-(R2032), no. 2.
4   As of 1986 Aruba has its own fiscal system and Curaçao and St. Maarten have copied the fiscal system from the Netherlands Antilles and subsequently adjusted this system at their own discretion. In this context it is relevant to mention that also within the Netherlands Antilles important differences existed between both islands.
5   Despite the fact that the new agreement, as well as the TRK, is a Dutch Kingdom Act, the agreement shows comparisons with a tax treaty.

may be different compared to the interests of St. Maarten. A potential downside is that each country had to negotiate separately with the Netherlands, while the three Caribbean countries could have taken a stronger position in the negotiations with the Netherlands if they had negotiated together.[6]

As a result of the choice for bilateral tax agreements during the Kingdom Conference on Fiscal Affairs in Aruba on 19 and 20 November 2009[7], the TRK will remain applicable in the fiscal relations between countries that have not agreed on bilateral tax agreements after the introduction of the Bilateral Tax Agreement Netherlands Curaçao (TANC), either temporarily or permanently. Meanwhile, the Netherlands has concluded a bilateral tax agreement with St. Maarten.[8] Besides, the Netherlands intends to conclude a bilateral agreement with Aruba.

The three Caribbean countries can choose whether they want to maintain the TRK between themselves, or if they want to agree upon new bilateral or multilateral agreements.

The immediate cause for the new tax agreement was, as mentioned, the constitutional amendments of the Kingdom of the Netherlands as a result of the discontinuation of the Netherlands Antilles. Curaçao and St. Maarten became autonomous countries within the Kingdom of the Netherlands (and the other islands: Bonaire, St. Eustatius and Saba, also collectively referred to as the BES islands, became public entities or special municipalities within the Netherlands). Besides for a longer time it had already been a wish from both parties to amend the TRK on a number of points. The Netherlands, for example, included in its tax treaty policy the desire to have taxation rights on pensions and

---

6   Roland Brandsma, Suniel Pancham, Hans Ruiter, Steve Vanenburg and Paul van Vliet, 'Caribische landen, werk samen', Het Financieele Dagblad of 1 December 2011.
7   Parliamentary Papers II 2013/14, 33 955-(R2032), no. 3, p. 1.
8   Dutch Government Gazette 2016, 21.

other payments which have been deducted from the Dutch taxable base during the accumulation phase. Curaçao also expressed the desire to amend the TRK. In particular the 8.3% dividend withholding tax rate resulted in a fiscal barrier for the financial sector. As a result of this dividend withholding tax rate it was difficult for Curaçao to compete with both offshore jurisdictions that do not levy taxes on income or profits as the Cayman Islands and Bermuda, as well as European countries that can receive dividend from Dutch residents companies exempted from dividend withholding tax under the Parent-Subsidiary Directive, such as Malta.

III. Main changes

At the time of shaping the Bilateral Tax Agreement Netherlands Curaçao (TANC) both the OECD MC[9][10] and the Dutch tax treaty policy have been taken into consideration.10[11] In section 4 we discuss the scope of the agreement, definition of residency as well as the new regime on hybrid entities. Subsequently the main changes relevant to actual practises are discussed: the dividend withholding tax (section 5), the substantial interest regime (section 6), the taxation of pensions (section 7) and the provision for gift tax and inheritance tax (section 8). In section 9, we briefly discuss a number of other changes. This article concludes with a comparison of the Tax Agreement Netherlands-St. Maarten (section 10) and a conclusion (section 11).

---

[9] The OECD-Model Convention is published by the Organisation for Economic Co-operation and Development. The last full version has been published on 22 July 2010. The last amendments have been published on 17 July 2012.

[10] Memorandum (policy note) on Dutch Tax Treaty Policy.

[11] Parliamentary Papers II 2013/14, 33 955-(R2032), no. 3, p. 2.

IV. Scope and residency

The agreement covers only taxes on income since both the Netherlands and Curaçao (no longer) levy taxes on capital gains. In addition, a fictitious tax residency provision is included in respect of the Dutch inheritance tax and gif tax. Residents of both countries have access to the agreement.[12] For purposes of the TANC the Netherlands also includes the BES islands.

A natural person who only has to pay taxes in one of the countries on income from that country will not qualify a resident of that country for purposes of the TANC. The usual tiebreaker rule of permanent home, centre of vital interests or habitual residence is applicable to individuals who are residents of both countries. Notwithstanding ordinary tax treaties, having the Dutch nationality has no distinctive meaning. Therefore, this condition is not included.

A legal entity is considered a resident of one of the countries in case the legal entity is established in the Netherlands for the purpose of corporate income tax and in Curaçao for the purpose of income tax.[13] An exemption is made in article 1 for the 'Stichting Particulier Fonds' (SPF), the trust, the (Curaçao) Vrijgestelde Vennootschap and the (Dutch) vrijgestelde beleggingsinstelling (VBI). They are excluded from certain provisions relating to dividends, interest, royalties, capital gains and provisions regarding residual income. Besides, the SPF and the trust may be entitled to such provisions provided that they have a status of special purpose assets, resulting in being subject to a profit tax in Curaçao.

Furthermore, it is remarkable that the usual provision regarding the effective place of management is not included for legal entities. If a legal entity qualifies as resident of both countries, the countries will mutually agree on the

---

[12] Article 1, paragraph 1 TANC.
[13] Article 4, paragraph 2 TANC.

deemed place of residence of this legal entity. Arbitrage is possible if the countries fail to agree. The explanatory notes indicate that the Netherlands aimed to raise a barrier with this provision against the movement of the effective place of management of a Dutch entity to Curaçao to avoid, for example, Dutch dividend withholding taxes. This place of residence provision is in line with the alternative provision of article 4, paragraph 3 OECD MC.[14] The Netherlands included this alternative provision in, amongst others, the tax treaties with the United Kingdom and the United States of America. This place of residence provision creates more uncertainty about the effective place of residence of legal entities for tax purposes. Aspects such as substance and business considerations clearly have to be taken into consideration in case of a proposed cross border transfer. These aspects also need to be taken into account by entities that are already established in Curaçao.

IV.1. Hybrid entities

The TANC contains specific rules for hybrid entities based on which the countries should enter into mutual consultation in order to avoid that these hybrid entities may be subject to double taxation or might not be subject to taxation at all.[15] The applicability of the TANC has explicitly been stated for a number of situations. In these situations, mutual consultation between the countries will not take place. In principle these rules determine that the source country follows the transparent or non-transparent qualification of a hybrid entity by the country of residence for tax purposes.[16] On condition that the income is treated as income of a resident in this country of residence.

---

[14] Paragraph 24.1 of the OECD commentary (2010) on article 4.
[15] Article 4, paragraph 6 TANC.
[16] Article 4, paragraph 7, subparagraph a TANC.

The explanatory notes mention certain examples. This can include, for example, dividends or profits obtained with a permanent establishment.

Example 1

Income flows from the Netherlands to an entity in Curaçao. This entity is regarded as a transparent entity in the Netherlands, but in Curaçao as non-transparent. One of the members of the entity lives in Curaçao. A second member lives in a third country. The Netherlands would, based on national law, not consider this entity as a resident of Curaçao. However, this hybrid entity is a resident of Curaçao and can therefore make direct appeal to article 4 TANC.

Example 2

Contrary to the first example, the entity is regarded as a non-transparent entity in the Netherlands, but in Curaçao as transparent. The entity is not subject to taxation in Curaçao. However the member is subject to taxation in Curaçao on the income attributable to this member. The Netherlands grants the member access to the TANC. From the explanatory notes it can be derived that the TANC is not applicable on income attributable to a resident of a third country. This is because a resident of a third party is not a resident of the Netherlands or Curaçao and the hybrid entity does not qualify as a resident for purposes of the TANC since it is not subject to taxation.[17]

---

[17] Article 4, paragraph 2, subparagraph b in conjunction with article 1, paragraph 1 TANC.

Example 3

Contrary to the second example, the entity is established in a third country. Curaçao levies taxes on income that is attributable to the member that is a resident of Curaçao. Therefore, the Netherlands applies the TANC to the income attributable to this member. The TANC is not applicable to income attributed to a resident of a third country.

Example 4

Different from the previous example, the entity is regarded transparent in the Netherlands, but non-transparent in Curaçao. In this case the TANC will not apply because, notwithstanding the fact that the Netherlands attributes the income to the resident of Curaçao based on its national laws, the entity is not subject to direct taxation and the entity is also not a resident of Curaçao. Obviously, these examples also apply in reversed situations in which Curaçao would be the source country and the Netherlands would be the country of residence.

Both the Netherlands and Curaçao could levy taxes based on their national law if income of an entity that is resident of the Netherlands is enjoyed by another entity that is also resident of the Netherlands and the members of the second entity are residents of Curaçao.[18] If the Netherlands would qualify the second entity as non-transparent, then the income would be attributed to that entity. Curaçao may also allocate the income to the members of the entity that are residents of Curaçao, if the entity is qualified as a transparent from a Curaçao perspective. However, in case the Netherlands would also qualify the second entity as transparent and Curaçao would qualify this entity as non-transparent, the Netherlands would allocate the income

---

18 Article 4, paragraph 7, subparagraph b TANC.

to the members in Curaçao and the TANC would apply. Curaçao would not directly levy taxes on the income but would levy tax at the moment the second entity would make a distribution. The outcome would be the same in the reverted situation with two Curaçao resident entities and members which are residents of the Netherlands.

One the one hand the first case could lead to double taxation if, for example, the second entity receives an interest payment. The Netherlands will levy taxes on the interest income at the level of the second entity, whilst Curaçao would levy taxes at the level of the members, without elimination of double taxation based on article 11 TANC. This article allocates the right to levy taxes on interest income to the country of residence.

On the other hand, the second case could lead to a double non-taxation if the Netherlands would not levy taxes on the interest income at the level of the second entity. Curaçao will not levy taxes on the interest income at the level of the member. If the Curaçao participation exemption applies to a subsequent distribution of the second entity, the interest income would remain fully untaxed.

In short, the source country will follow the (non)-transparent qualification of an entity by the receiving country, provided that the entity is a resident of that country. However, if the entity is a resident of a third state, the source country will only follow the (non)-transparent qualification of the member resident of or established in that other country. The qualification of the third state will not be followed if the receiving entity is based in the source country. The starting point seems not to be if a cross-border payment occurs from a fiscal perspective, but if a cross-border payment occurs from a civil law perspective. In case a cross-border payments occurs from a civil law perspective, efforts have been made to prevent double taxation and double non-taxation. If this is not the case, the source country has the right to apply its national rules.

V. Dividend withholding taxes

The new provisions with respect to the taxation of dividends is expected to be, in practice, of great importance. Based on the regulation that was in force from 2001 to 2015, 8,3% dividend withholding tax was withheld on dividends that were distributed from entities resident in the Netherlands to entities resident in Curaçao, provided that the Curaçao resident held an interest of at least 25%. In a few cases dividend distributions remain fully untaxed based on the text of article 10 TANC. If the conditions for the application of the 0% rate are not met, the dividend withholding tax rate amounts 15%. As a transitional provision applies for existing structures.

Until 2019, the year in which also the transitional provision of the old Curaçao offshore regime will end, a rate of 5% applies under the transitional provision. One comment which could be made is that this provision only applies to dividend distributions from a Dutch tax perspective, since there is no taxation on dividends in Curaçao.

In order to be able to apply the 0% rate, a few conditions need to be met. Article 10, paragraph 4 TANC defines the so called "Limitations on Benefits" (LOB). The LOB-provisions in the TANC seem in accordance with the concept LOB-provisions of BEPS Action 6,[19] as a result of the Action Plan on Base Erosion and Profit Shifting of the OECD.[20] What is striking is that the LOB-provision of the TANC does not contain a provision for algemeen nut beogende instellingen (charitable or public benefit organizations), unlike the concept LOB-provisions of Action 6.[21]

---

[19] Action 6, www.oecd.org/ctp/beps-2015-final-reports.htm.
[20] OECD (2013), Action Plan on Base Erosion and Profit Shifting, OECD Publishing, www.oecd.org/ctp/BEPSActionPlan.pdf.
[21] Discussion Draft Action 6, p. 6.

The 0% rate applies to pension funds and state institutions. Besides, the 0% rate applies to an entity that holds an interest of at least 10% (a relaxation of the previous condition of 25%) in an entity resident in the other state that distributes dividends, provided that one or more of the following conditions are met:

- it is listed on a recognized stock exchange;
- the principal class of the shares is owned by listed entities;
- it functions as headquarter company for a multinational corporate group;
- it employs at least three qualified persons;
- it is engaged in the active conduct of a trade or business, but it employs less than three qualified persons and the dividend relates to the active conduct of a trade or business;
- has real activities, but it employs less than three qualified persons and on request the competent authority of the state in which the income arises determines that the main purpose of the incorporation and continuation of the company or ownership of a shareholding is not to qualify for the benefits of the TANC;
- more than 50% of the aggregate vote and value of all it shares is owned, directly or indirectly, by natural persons who are resident of either the Netherlands or Curaçao.

An exemption to this provision applies to the BES islands. If the entity that distributes the dividend is a resident of one of the BES islands, a tax rate of 5% applies in all cases.[22] The explanatory notes mention that this is because the 'opbrengstbelasting', together with the taxation on real estate, have been introduced as a substitution of the profit tax. The opbrengstbelasting should function as a

---

[22] Article 10, paragraph 10 TANC.

"robust fence of 5% taxation around the Caribbean part of the Netherlands"[23] that could not be reduced with the use of an (international) participation. This argument would be understandable if also permanent establishment on the BES islands would be subject to the opbrengstbelasting. This is however not the case. The legislator made a conscious decision to not include profits of a permanent establishments of an entity that is not a resident of the BES islands in the taxable base at the time of adopting the Belastingwet BES.[24] According to the lawmaker in such a case taxation on real estate would be sufficient. From that point of view the exclusion of the opbrengstbelasting in article 10 TANC can be questioned.

V.1. Listed entities

The condition of being listed, as mentioned in article 10, paragraph 4, subparagraph a TANC, can be fulfilled either direct or indirect. The 0% rate will be applicable if the receiving entity is a resident of Curaçao, is listed on a recognized stock exchange and is regularly traded on one or more recognized stock exchanges.

The 0% rate is also applicable if more than 50% of the aggregate vote and value of all of the shares is directly owned by one or more listed entities, provided that one of the following conditions is met. The listed shareholder needs to be:

1. resident of the Netherlands or Curaçao; or
2. resident of another country that has concluded a bilateral tax treaty with the Netherlands on which basis the Netherlands should apply the 0% rate, or both countries are part of a multilateral agreement on which basis the Netherlands should apply the 0% rate. This is,

---

23 (R2032), no. 3, p. 23.
24 Parliamentary Papers II 2009/10, 32 189, no. 7, p. 17.

for example, the case if the shareholder is a resident of one of the EU Member States and the conditions of the Parent-Subsidiary Directive are met. The term recognized stock exchange means any stock exchange registered in a EU member state, the Dutch Caribbean Securities Exchange (DCSX) established in Curaçao, the NASDAC and any stock exchange registered with the Securities Exchange Commission as a national securities exchange for purposes of the Securities Exchange Act of 1934, the stock exchange of Bolsa Mexicana de Valores in Mexico and the Toronto Stock Exchange, the Chilean Bolsa de Comercio, Bolsa Electrónica de Chile and Bolsa de Corredores. This list can be expanded by mutual agreement between the Netherlands and Curaçao.

V.2. Headquarter company

The 0% rate can also be applied in case the entity that is based in Curaçao functions as headquarter company for a multinational corporate group. The following conditions need to be met in accordance with article 10, paragraph 4, subparagraph b TANC. The headquarter company based in Curaçao may not benefit from any special tax regimes for financial services, royalty payments or insurance activities. Besides, the headquarter company needs to have independent responsibility regarding the control or finance activities of the group. Also the group entities are engaged in an active business in at least five countries and the business activities carried in each of the five countries generate at least 10% of the gross income of the group. The business activities carried on in the country of the company that distributes the dividend should generate less than 50% of the gross income.

To meet the condition, the in entity established in Curaçao should have sufficient expertise, which implies that it needs to employ qualified persons sufficiently qualified to carry out their tasks properly.[25]

The head office may not be subject to any special regime that exclusively applies to entities that perform financial services. The Curaçao participation exemption is not regarded as a special regime, even if it differs on certain point from the Dutch participation exemption. Besides, Curaçao maintains an export regime from 1 January 2014 onwards. This export regime is applicable on a broad range of activities, provided that they are 90% or more focused on foreign countries. [26] Unlike the earlier offshore regime, no limitation apply to the users of this regime.

V.3. At least three qualified employees

The 0% rate can only be applied if, according to article 10, paragraph 4, subparagraph c TANC, the Curaçao entity employs at least three qualified persons. This condition is comparable with the fictitious place of establishment provision as mentioned in article 5.2 of the Belastingwet BES.[27] The headquarter company criteria do not clarify the required qualifications. The "at least three qualified employees" condition is further explained with the requirement that the employees should be able to independently look after the activities of the entity. They should have tasks and responsibilities within the framework of the normal corporate involvement. The Explanatory Memorandum states that the employees should at least be able and have the responsibility to control the following assets: investments, participations, fluid assets, assets that are dis-

---

25 Parliamentary Papers II 2013/14, 33 955-(R2032), no. 3, p. 37.
26 Article 9 Landsverordening op de winstbelasting 1940, applicable from 1 January 2014. Based on this regime an effective profit tax rate of 4% applies to qualifying entities.
27 (R2032), no. 3, p. 38.

posed and loans. It will not be sufficient to hire qualified employees from, for example, a trust office. However, it is not required that each employee has the same expertise. Together the employees should be qualified to look after the activities of the entity. Therefore, this requirement seems an interesting possibility to qualify for the exemption.

This possibility can, for example, apply if the entity established in Curaçao would not qualify as headquarter company because the group is not active in at least five countries or because the entity still uses the old offshore regime until 2019 or benefits from any special tax regimes for financial services, royalty payments or insurance activities.

V.4. Business participation

If the Dutch participation runs an active business and this participation is attributable to the business activities of the shareholder in Curaçao, then the 0% rate is applicable based on article 10, paragraph 5, subparagraph a TANC. Investing in shares or managing such investments for one's own account are excluded from the qualification under this provision, unless it concerns a bank, an insurance company or a stockbroker. This provision can be relevant if, for example, the headquarter group requirement is not met and there are neither three qualified employees. This provision contains a more relaxed substance requirement, which can be relevant for smaller companies. However, for such companies, the presence of qualified employees must be appropriate for the size of the company.

This provision can also be applied if the entity in Curaçao is an intermediate holding of a foreign parent company, the business activities of the participation are in line with the business activities of the parent, and the Curaçao intermediate holding fulfills a linking-function (i.e. schakelfunctie). The intermediate holding in Curaçao can also fulfill a linking-function if the parent company is a top holding that fulfills an essential function in the business activities of the group and the participation runs an active business. The comparison between the socalled linking-function for the application of the Dutch participation exemption and the foreign tax liability in case of a substantial interest is remarkable.

V.5. Safety net clause

Lastly, a safety net clause has been included in article 10, paragraph 5, subparagraph b TANC. If the previous requirements are not met, the 0% rate could still be applicable based on the safety net clause. The safety net clause might apply if the government of the source country (i.e. the Netherlands) determines that both the entity in Curaçao the Dutch participation are not established, maintained or acquired with the main purpose or one of the main purposes to become eligible to the 0% rate. The parliamentary proceedings[28] indicate that the Netherlands requires that certain substance requirements are met next to the requirement that the shares belong to the business capital of a Curaçao resident entity. The Netherlands takes into account the substance requirements that are applied in assessing an advance tax ruling request of a Dutch entity.[29] In the annex of the so-called Advanced Tax Ruling (ATR) Decree, various minimum requirements are mentioned. Based on these requirements at least half of the statutory members of the board of directors in Curaçao, with a right to take decisions, should be residents of or established in Curaçao. In addition, they should be sufficiently qualified to carry out their tasks properly. Their tasks should at least concern decision-making, under the responsibility of the entity and within the framework of the normal corporate involvement, on transactions concluded by the

---

28 Parliamentary Papers II 2013/14, 33 955-(R2032), no. 3, p. 38.
29 Decree of 3 June 2014, no. DGB 2014/3099, Stcrt. 2014, 15956.

entity, including the proper completion of concluded transactions. Furthermore, amongst others, the most important bank account of the entity must be held in Curaçao, the bookkeeping should take place in Curaçao and the entity is, by its best knowledge, not (also) a tax residents of any other state.

In order to apply the safety net clause, a request must be filed with the APA-/ATR-team of the Dutch tax authorities/Large Businesses (office Rotterdam). Clearly, there should be sufficient substance in Curaçao. If, for example, (part) of the board decisions are taken in the Netherlands, then the request for the application of article 10, paragraph 6 TANC can be denied. Besides, during bilateral consultations the Netherlands could claim that the entity is a fiscal resident of the Netherlands on the basis of article 4, paragraph 5 TANC. It remains to be seen if fulfilling the minimum requirements in the ATR-Decree will be enough to qualify for the safety net clause. Experience has shown that the ATR-team does not takes for granted that the shares belong to the business capital of the shareholder.

V.6. Natural persons

The last possibility to qualify for the 0% rate arises if the shares of the Curaçao resident entity are for at least 50% held by natural persons who are residents of the Netherlands or Curaçao. The explanatory notes mention that article 17, paragraph 3, subparagraph a Dutch Corporate Income Tax Act 1969 (DCITA) can be applicable in abusive situations from a Dutch tax perspective. In such case, the Curaçao resident entity shall be subjected to Dutch corporate income tax as a foreign taxpayer on the basis of the substantial interest rules (i.e. aanmerkelijkbelangregeling), or the so-called 'technical AB'. According to the explanatory memorandum, this might occur if the existing structure is modified by placing a Curaçao holding entity between the Dutch entity and the Curaçao natural person.[30] However, this might not occur if a resident of Curaçao acquires a participation in a Dutch company (a newly established structure) with the use of the Curaçao holding entity.

In the explanatory memorandum of this provision, the following remark is made: "For completeness sake, it is noted that, as a consequence of the first paragraph of article 22 of the provision for abuse situations, from a Dutch perspective article 17, paragraph 3, subparagraph b DCITA could apply. One can think of the situation in which one or more natural persons interpose an entity that meets the ownership requirement to be entitled to the exemption of source taxation."

From 1 January 2016, the Netherlands has amended article 17, paragraph 3, subparagraph b DCITA. The Curaçao entity can be included in the Dutch corporate tax base if it holds an interest in the Dutch entity with the main purpose or one of the main purposes to avoid the levy of Dutch personal income tax or Dutch dividend withholding tax at the level of another taxpayer and there is an arrangement or series of arrangements which are considered wholly artificial (i.e. not put into place for valid commercial reasons which reflect economic reality). Valid commercial reasons may exist if, for example, the Curaçao entity is an intermediate holding company linking between the ultimate holding company and the business and in addition meets certain minimum substance requirements in Curaçao as mentioned in section 5.

Interposing an entity is also relevant for the applicability of article 1, paragraph 7 Dutch Dividend Withholding Tax Act 1966 (DDWTA). Article 10, paragraph 8 TANC would result in a dead letter as a consequence of the applicability of article 1, paragraph 7 DDWTA. It would do the legislator well if he would further elaborate on the scope of article 10, paragraph 8 TANC.

---

30 (R2032), no. 3, p. 39.

There seem to be no abuse in the case a resident of the Netherlands migrates to Curaçao taking along his or her Dutch holding entity. In that case, the migration of the Dutch holding entity is not motivated by, for example, Dutch dividend withholding tax avoidance purposes, but motivated by the wish of the shareholder to execute the effective management from Curaçao. However, this provision is not completely clear. Article 22, paragraph 2 TANC excludes the application of the anti-abuse provision in case the Curaçao entity is entitled to the 0% rate on the basis of article 10, paragraph 3 or 5 TANC. However, article 22, paragraph 2 TANC does not exclude the application of the anti-abuse provision in case article 10, paragraph 8 TANC would be applicable. This is remarkable because if the entity is entitled to the 0% rate on the basis of the third or fifth paragraph, the eight paragraph would be unnecessary. If the 0% rate would apply based on the eight paragraph, the Netherlands would be able to apply its foreign substantial interest rules of article 17, paragraph three, subparagraph b DCITA on the basis of article 22, paragraph 2 TANC. The NOB asked in its commentary, sent to the Finance Committee of the House of Representatives, an explanation why article 10, paragraph 8 TANC is not also included in the exclusion of the anti-abuse provision as mentioned in article 22, paragraph 2 TANC.[31] According to the legislator, article 10, paragraph 8 TANC was included at the request of Curaçao.[32] It has been recognized that article 10, paragraph 8 TANC could lead to the avoidance of dividend withholding tax. Article 17, paragraph 3, subparagraph b DCITA remains, according to the legislator, intentionally applicable to dividends. Therefore, article 10 paragraph 8 BNC has limited meaning in practice.

---

[31] Commentary of the Commissie Wetsvoorstellen of the Nederlandse Orde van Belastingadviseurs, 1 July 2014.
[32] Parliamentary Papers II 2014/15, 33 955-(R2032), no. 6, p. 20.

V.7. Transitional provisions

It is expected that part of the existing Curaçao-Dutch structures would not qualify for the 0% rate. In those cases, a transitional provision is included in article 30 TANC. The application of this provision requires that the entity was already a resident of Curaçao before 5 June 2014 (the date when the legislation proposal was sent to the House of Representatives). In addition, the entity needs to hold an interest of at least 25% in an entity established in the Netherlands. On the basis of the transitional provision, a reduced rate of 5% instead of the old rate of 8,3% applies up to and including 2019. Thereafter, the general rate of 15% will be applicable to these entities. Besides dividends, article 30 BNC is also applicable to capital gains. Article 30 paragraph, 2 TANC states that article 17 paragraph, 3 subparagraph b DCITA does not apply in cases that are covered by the transitional provision.[33] The transitional provision ends on the same date as the transitional provision of the Curaçao offshore regime, which also expires in 2019.[34]

VI. Income from substantial interest

Next to the changes regarding the dividend withholding tax article, there are also important changes for direct shareholdings of natural persons in entities in the other state. One can think of residents of the Netherlands that moved to Curaçao, whether or not taking along their company.

The TANC limits the taxation of dividends and profit distributions to 15%. Only benefits from the disposal of shares or profit participations certificates that belong to a substantial interest could be subject to taxation in the

---

[33] Parliamentary Papers II 2013/14, 33 955-(R2032), no. 7, p. 7-8.
[34] Article VI, P.B. 1999, nr. 244, after the amendments mentioned in P.B. 2001, nr. 145.

Netherlands at a maximum rate of 25% for a period of five years after the emigration.[35] Besides, a protective tax assessment can be issued by the Dutch tax authorities as a result of an emigration from the Netherlands which also can be recovered by the Dutch tax authorities after a period of five years after the emigration.

The TANC extends the possibilities of the Netherlands to effectuate a substantial interest tax claim compared to the TRK. The Netherlands might apply the Dutch tax rate on both profit distributions[36] and capital gains[37] until ten years after emigration, as long as it concerns an increase in value that was already present at the time of emigration. In this way, the Netherlands has secured its national tax rate of a maximum of 25% on both capital gains and dividend distributions.

Curaçao levies taxes on income from substantial interest against a tax rate of 19,5%.[38][39] The TRK allowed Curaçao to levy additional taxes from 15% to 19,5%. Under the TANC, Curaçao has no room for their own additional taxation after the tax credit for the Dutch taxation. In the reversed situation (i.e. a resident of Curaçao migrates to the Netherlands) Curaçao has the right to levy taxation against a tax rate of 19,5% in that same period of ten years. However, the Netherlands would be able to levy additional taxes which shall not exceed its national rate of a maximum of 25%.

Also in this case a transitional provision applies. Whoever migrated to Curaçao respectively the Netherlands before 5 June 2014 can only be followed by the previous country of resident state a maximum of five years.

---

[35] Article 2.12 Dutch Income Tax Act 2001.
[36] Article 10, paragraph 14 TANC.
[37] Article 13, paragraph 5 TANC.
[38] Article 24, paragraph 3, Landsverordening op de inkomstenbelasting 1943.
[39] Memorandum (policy note) on Dutch Tax Treaty Policy, p. 54.

During this period, the higher income tax rate is applicable to dividends instead of the withholding tax rate of 15%. Nevertheless, the previous mentioned time period of 10 years is applicable to a disposal in case a protective tax assessment has been issued.

VII. Pensions and Annuities

Internationally it is standard practice to allocate the right to levy taxes on pensions to the country of residence with the exception of state pensions and commuted pensions. The Netherlands included in its tax treaty policy39 the desire to have taxation rights on pensions and other payments which have been deducted from the Dutch taxable base during the accumulation phase. By way of a fiscal compromise it can be agreed that states will share the right to levy taxes. This Dutch tax treaty policy has been expressed in article 17 TANC, although this tax treaty policy differs from article 18 OECD MC. Under this new provision the Netherlands and Curaçao are entitled to levy taxes which shall not exceed 15 per cent on private pension installments paid from the source country. The country of residence also has the right to levy taxes, however the country of residence should allow a deduction on the income taxes of that resident levied in the source country. The scope of this provision has been extended to tax facilitated annuity installments. The source state maintains the right to levy taxes on commuted pension.

Also the allocation of taxation rights on state pension (article 18, paragraph 3 TANC) remains unchanged. The right to levy taxes on social security benefits changes. Contrary to the BRK the TANC contains a social security provision. Based on this social security provision the taxing right on the Dutch WAO-uitkering are also allocated to the source country. A Transitional provision applies. Article 29

TANC provides that article 17 TANC does not apply to payments of periodic installments that have already started on 5 June 2014 to a person who was a resident of Curaçao or the Netherlands on that date.

VIII. Inheritance tax and gift tax

The inheritance tax and gift tax have been one of the provisions of the BRK that the Netherlands preferred to change. Under the TANC the Netherlands is entitled to levy taxes on donations until one year after emigration. In the event of death the right to levy a taxes expires the day after emigration.[40] The TANC extends the right to levy taxes to 5 years both in the case of inheritance taxes and gift taxes.[41] A transactional provision applies, just like the previously mentioned transactional provisions related to the extension of Dutch taxation rights.[42] Based on this transitional provision the term of one year in case of gift taxes and one day in case of inheritance taxes would remain in place for those who were a resident of Curaçao on 5 June 2014. This transactional provision only applies to natural persons who migrated from the Netherlands to Curaçao, in alignment with the transactional provisions applicable to pensions and annuities. This restriction raised no objection because Curaçao tax legislation does not include the possibility to follow someone for purposes of levying gift taxes and inheritance taxes after emigration.

---

[40] Article 29 TANC.
[41] Article 28 TANC includes a fictitious place of residence.
[42] Article 31 TANC.

IX. Other changes

We will mention certain other changes which are included in the TANC hereafter.

IX.1. Permanent establishment for services

Based on the TRK a permanent establishment exists in case activities are carried out for at least 183 days. The TANC extends the scope of the provision with services. A permanent establishment is assumed to exist if activities are carried out or services are provided during more than 183 days within a timeframe of twelve months. In such a case the right to levy taxes is allocated to source country. It is irrelevant if one person is present in a country for more than 183 days or multiple persons are one by one present in a country for more than 183 days within a period of twelve months. The activities, however, should be carried out or services should be provided with respect to one project. If an employee, for example, carries out activities for two different project and therefore the employee is present in that country two period of four months within a timeframe of twelve months, a permanent establishment will not exist.

IX.2. Entertainers and Sportspersons

Entertainers and sportspersons earn business income through a permanent establishment in the source country by fiction based on article 9 TANC. Article 15 TANC should be applied in case of an employment relationship. However, article 16 TANC provides a general provision for entertainers and sportspersons. The source country has the right to levy taxes regardless if the income is earned by an independent entertainer/sportsperson or an employed entertainer/sportsperson.

This provision (that does not exist in the Dutch tax treaty policy) is adopted at the request of Curaçao.[43] Although the Netherlands does not levy taxes on entertainers and sportspersons who perform their activities in an employment relationship[44] this will not result in double non-taxation, because Curaçao only allows a deduction.

IX.3. Interest and royalties

Article 12 TANC contains a provision in conformity with the OECD MC. In case a remuneration is considered too high compared to the at arm's length remuneration, article 12 TANC only applies to the at arm's length remuneration. The excess may be taxed by both countries based on their national legislation.

IX.4. Information exchange

Both countries will exchange information according to international standards. Given recent developments in the OECD this is expected to mean that information will not only be shared upon request but also spontaneously and even automatically.

IX.5. Anti-abuse

Article 22 TANC, the anti-abuse provision, entitles countries the right to apply their national anti-abuse provisions in case of fraud, abuse and improper use. An exception is made for article 17, paragraph 3, subparagraph b DCITA in case a resident of Curaçao is entitled to the dividend withholding tax rate of 0% on the basis of article 10 TANC. Also an anti-abuse rule applies in the context of the so called safety net clause of article 10, paragraph 5 TANC (as

---

43 Parliamentary Papers II 2013/14, 33 955-(R2032), no. 3, p. 43.
44 Article 7.2, paragraph 2 Dutch Income Tax Act 2001.

discussed in section 5.5). Based on the safety net clause the government of the source state could determine that the main purpose or one of the main purposes of the Curaçao entity is to become eligible to the 0% rate.

IX.6. Non-discrimination

The non-discrimination provision of article 23 TANC largely corresponds to article 24 of the OECD MC. Article 23 TANC differs to a considerable degree from the TRK with respect to natural persons. Article 39 TRK includes a provision which stipulates that a natural person should be entitled to the same benefits in the source country which apply to residents of that source country. Based on that provision a resident of the Netherlands, for example, was entitles to the same tax free threshold for income tax purposes as a resident of Curaçao. Therefore, the tax burden on income from the Netherlands increases under the TANC. The Netherlands does not grant a tax credit to foreign taxpayers in both the European part as the BES islands. Consequently, under the TANC the tax burden increases for residents of Curaçao who lived in the Netherlands for several years and as such receive a Dutch state pension. Previously these state pensions were largely untaxed in the Netherlands while Curaçao allowed a proportional deduction. The latter remains the same, however taxes should be paid in the Netherlands due to the introduction of article 23 TANC. A transitional provision applies to persons who already received state pension and lived in Curaçao on 5 June 2015.

The provision of article 40 TRK which provides a reduction in taxation for charitable or public benefit organizations is maintained and can now be found in article 23, paragraph 7 TANC.

X. Tax Agreement between the Netherlands and St. Maarten

As from January 2014 the negotiations between the Netherlands and St. Maarten intensified after completion of
the discussions between the Netherlands and Curaçao in
December 2013. The TANC served as starting point for the
Tax Agreement between the Netherlands and St. Maarten
(TANSM).[45] Therefore, the content of the TANSM almost
entirely corresponds to the TANC. Also the transitional
provisions of the TANSM correspond to the TANC. Existing structures which do not qualify for the 0% rate have
been granted a delay which includes a tax rate of 5% until
2019.

As of 1 March 2016 the TANSM has come into effect.
The TANSM applies to fiscal years and fiscal periods starting on or after 1 January 2017. In case of taxes withheld at
source, the new agreement is applicable to payments made
on or after 1 January 2017.

XI. Conclusion

The new Tax Agreement between the Netherlands and
Curaçao (TANC) has finally entered into force. After years
of amendments of the TRK the agreement between the two
countries is now completely revised. The agreement finally
contains the long-awaited introduction of a 0% rate applicable to qualifying cross-border dividend distributions. Fifteen years after the introduction of the Nieuw Fiscaal
Raamwerk (NFR) the anticipated objective is achieved with
the application of a Limitations on Benefits provision.

---

[45] Parliamentary Papers II 2014/15, 34 263-(R2055), no. 3, p. 2-3.

Existing structures that do not qualify for the 0% tax rate have been granted a delay based on transitional provisions which include a tax rate of 5% until 2019. It is expected that structures that cannot make the adjustments will look for alternatives outside Curaçao. By means of this new tax agreement Curaçao finally moves away from the old offshore regime. The question is now if the TANC is sufficient to further strengthen the ties between the Netherlands and Curaçao. This will not entirely depend on the TANC. Curaçao has concluded multiple tax information exchange agreements. Furthermore, from 1 September 2013 on Curaçao participates in the Convention on Mutual Administrative Assistance in Tax Matters.[46] This makes clear that Curaçao fully endorses the current trend towards transparency. Good cooperation between the Netherlands and Curaçao on the bases of the TANC should be beneficial for both countries. It has to be seen if this would compensate losses with respect to old structures in place until 2019. These considerations are of lesser importance to St. Maarten which did not have an extensive off-shore industry like Curaçao.

---

[46] www.oecd.org/ctp/exchange-of-tax-information/Status_of_convention.pdf.

2

Dutch Caribbean Islands

MR. HANS RUITER • MS. SANDY VAN THOL

I. Introduction

In this chapter, only the corporate income tax of the different jurisdictions will be discussed. In addition, the fiscal relationships between the various jurisdictions will be discussed. Please note that the details of the various tax systems will not always be explained. Instead, the focus will be on the differences and similarities between the various tax systems. The discussion of the tax systems itself will be in principle high level and only more detailed if the context requires this.

First, a short introduction of the Kingdom of the Netherlands is discussed. Subsequently, in each paragraph the various Dutch Caribbean islands are discussed from a tax perspective.

The islands of the Dutch Caribbean in principle each have their own tax system, except the BES islands. The BES islands (i.e. Bonaire, Sint Eustatius and Saba) in essence have the same tax system with only minor differences between the islands. For that purpose, only the tax system of Bonaire will be discussed.

Subsequently, the tax systems of Curaçao and Aruba will be discussed in each chapter. Please note that the tax system of Sint Maarten is very similar to the tax system of Curaçao and will not be discussed separately.

I.1 Kingdom of the Netherlands: a short introduction

1.1.1. General

To understand the fiscal relationships within the Kingdom of the Netherlands one must have a basic understanding of how the Kingdom of the Netherlands functions and how the internal relationships within the Kingdom of the Netherlands are arranged.

The internal relationship between the countries of the Kingdom of the Netherlands (hereafter: "the Kingdom") is regulated by the Statute of the Kingdom of the Netherlands[1] (December 15, 1954) (hereafter: "the Statute"). The philosophy behind the Statute is that all countries within the Kingdom are equal. Before and during World War II the Dutch Government started thinking differently about its relationship with its overseas territories and the Dutch Government wanted to grant more autonomy to its overseas territories (at that time still considered as "colonies"). This resulted in the Statute in 1954. After the Statute took effect the Kingdom consisted of 3 countries: The Netherlands, Surinam and the Netherlands Antilles (consisting of 6 Caribbean islands). In 1975 Surinam became independent and was no longer part of the Kingdom, leaving 2 countries within the Kingdom: The Netherlands and the Netherlands Antilles.

On January 1, 1986 Aruba became an independent country within the Kingdom of The Netherlands after a long period of discussions and negotiations between The Netherlands and Aruba by the political leaders of the respective countries at that time. In 2010 another constitutional change took place within the Kingdom. As of October 10, 2010 ("10-10-10") Bonaire, Saba and Sint Eustatius became part of The Netherlands as special municipalities (in Dutch: "openbare lichamen") in the sense of article 134

---

[1]   Staatsblad 2010, nr. 333.

of the Constitution of the Kingdom of the Netherlands. Also on that date Curaçao and Sint Maarten became countries within the Kingdom, like Aruba. Therefore as of October 10, 2010 the Kingdom consists of 4 countries: The Netherlands (including the BES-islands), Aruba, Curaçao and Sint Maarten[2].

I.1.2. Structure of the Kingdom

As of 1954 the Kingdom has the form of a federation of countries. As with every federation, there must be a clear definition of the authority of the federation and the member states. The member states are granted as much autonomy as possible and the federation should only look after the affairs of the Kingdom as a whole. The structure that is chosen for the Kingdom is that of the Statute as highest legal regulation and the Constitutions of the member states (The Netherlands, Sint Maarten, Curaçao and Aruba) as legal regulations that are of a lower legal order as the Statute.

The Statute is therefore the highest legal regulation of the Kingdom and as such has preference over the Constitution of The Netherlands (in Dutch: "Grondwet") and the Constitutions of Sint Maarten, Curaçao and Aruba (in Dutch: "Staatsregeling")[3]. According to the Statute, all the countries, which form part of the Kingdom of the Netherlands (The Netherlands (including BES-islands), Sint Maarten, Curaçao and Aruba, are responsible for their own internal affairs[4]. Kingdom affairs are taken care of jointly by the Kingdom government[5]. Kingdom affairs are, for example: defence, citizenship and foreign affairs. Fundamental human rights and general principles of good governance are regulated in the Statute and as such are guaranteed for

---

[2] Article 1, paragraph 1 Statute.
[3] Article 5, paragraph 2 Statute.
[4] Article 41, paragraph 1 Statute.
[5] Article 3 Statute.

all the member states (article 43 of the Statute). Article 2 of the Statute arranges the principle of Ministerial responsibility. Article 46 of the Statute arranges the principle of general voting rights.

Kingdom laws (in Dutch: "Rijkswetten") apply to the Kingdom as a whole (an example of a Kingdom law is the Tax Regulation for the Kingdom which will be discussed later). Other matters are regulated at the level of each individual country within the Kingdom. Taxation is – for example – a matter that is the responsibility of each individual country. Governors represent the King of the Kingdom in each of the countries of the Kingdom in which the King does not reside. The King appoints and dismisses the Governors[6].

I.2. Corporate Income Tax at Domestic level

I.2.1. Active income

I.2.1.1. Business Profits

I.2.1.1.1. BES islands
Profit tax on the BES-islands was abolished as of January 1, 2011. It was replaced by the property tax and the revenue tax[7]. The reason to abolish profit tax on the BES islands was that at the time of the constitutional reform (10-10-10) the profit tax revenue was approximately USD 3.2 million[8]. This revenue was considered too low to justify the administrative burden for companies to comply with the profit tax regulations and the burden for the tax authorities to execute the profit tax regulations. To avoid abuse of the absence of profit tax on the BES islands, specific anti-abuse regulations

---

[6] Article 2, paragraph 3 Statute.
[7] Explanatory Notes Tax Law BES, page 13.
[8] Explanatory Notes Tax Law BES, page 43.

apply. Based on the anti-abuse regulations, companies are considered to be established in The Netherlands, unless the companies (i) are admitted to a trade or service warehouse or (ii) by decision of the tax inspector are considered to be established on the BES islands (certain conditions apply for this decision).

I.2.1.1.2. Curaçao

The normal corporate income tax rate is applicable to all business income. Some types of income or some kinds of companies, are exempted or taxed at a lower tax rate based on a special regime. If the normal CIT regime applies, the business income, after offset of losses, is taxable at a rate of 22%.

I.2.1.1.2.1. Taxable event and taxable basis

Definition of profit

Article 3 of the State Ordinance Profit Tax describes the way the taxable profit of a company must be determined. Profit is determined based on sound business practice (in Dutch: "goed koopmans gebruik"). The profit must be determined consistently, independent from the expected outcome (in Dutch: "bestendige gedragslijn"). The way the profit is determined can only be changed if sound business practice justifies this.

Since sound business practice is not a clear and concrete definition of the way profit must be determined, in practice there can discussion about the explanation of sound business practice. Sound business practice is an old concept from Dutch tax law. Therefore there is a lot, very old but also recent jurisprudence regarding sound business practice. The concept of sound business practice is still developing and changing, based on new insights, changes in accounting principles and introduction of new products and industries.

Starting point for the determination of the fiscal profit are the commercial financial statements. This was decided by the Dutch Supreme Court in 1957[9]. The Supreme Court decided that the commercial financial statement should be followed for the determination of the fiscal profit, unless application of tax law or general tax principles would lead to a difference between the commercial and fiscal profit. Although officially Dutch Supreme court decisions regarding Dutch tax law have no relevance in Curaçao, in practice the Supreme Court decisions are followed.

Important tax principles which are used in sound business practice are:

- Matching principle (costs are allocated to the period in which the income is recognized)
- Reality principle (income and costs should be in accordance with the facts)
- Caution principle (unrealized profits are not taken into account, unrealized losses can – under certain conditions (brick judgment) be taken into account)
- Simplicity principle
- Consistency principle (a change of tax accounting principles is not allowed unless sound business practice allows the change[10])

An important decision regarding sound business practice is the decision of August 26, 1998[11] of the Dutch Supreme Court. Until that date a provision could only be formed if a legal obligation existed on balance date based on which the future payments should be made. The Supreme

---

9   BNB 1957/208.
10   Article 4, paragraph 5 SOPT
11   BNB 1998/409

Court decided that this condition no longer applied but that a provision could be formed if the following 3 conditions were met:

- Provision is based on facts and circumstances which occurred before balance date
- Costs can be allocated to the period before balance date (matching principle)
- There is reasonable certainty that the costs will occuur

Further definition of profit

If a company ceases to realize profits in Curaçao, it is taxable for the difference in fiscal book value and the market value of its assets at the moment the company terminates its activities[12]. This also applies if the companies conducts its business through a permanent establishment in Curaçao and assets are transferred from this permanent establishment[13].

Exemptions

Article 2 of the State Ordinance profit tax grants exemptions to various types of activities. Some important tax exemptions are:

1. A profit tax exemption for pension funds, savings funds, reservation funds, funeral funds, bad health funds and support funds for personnel or former personnel;
2. A profit tax exemption for the so-called trust or private foundation[14], unless the profit is realized with business activities.

---

12 Article 4, paragraph 3 SOPT.
13 Article 4, paragraph 4 SOPT.
14 Article 1, paragraph 1, letters I and j SOPT.

Deductions

Deductible costs

Costs which have to be made to realize the profit can be deducted from the profit. Furthermore assets can be depreciated for tax purposes if the assets have a certain economic life. If after the economic life, the asset still has a residual value, this must be taken into account for the calculation of the depreciation[15].

Investment allowance[16]

If a Curaçao company invests more than Awg 5,000 in assets, the investing company can claim an investment allowance of 10%. Investment allowance is a deduction on the taxable profit of a company. If – for example – a company invests for Awg 100,000, it can deduct 10% of Awg 100,000 is Awg 6,000 from its taxable profit. So if the taxable profit before the investment allowance is Awg 20,000, after deduction of the investment allowance the taxable profit is Awg 10,000.

Certain items do not qualify for investment allowance, like ground and animals.

Capital disposal charge[17]

If an asset is sold within 6 years (for buildings 15 years) after the start of the year the investment allowance was claimed, a capital disposal charge must be paid on the selling price. The capital disposal charge is 10% on the selling price.

---

[15] Article 5 SOPT.
[16] Article 5A SOPT.
[17] Article 5A, paragraph 2 SOPT.

Limitation of deduction of costs[18]

Certain costs are not or not completely deductible from the taxable profit of a company. First of all interest – including costs and exchange rate results – and remunerations for the use of goods are not deductible if paid to an entity which belongs to the same group of entities or a substantial interest shareholder, in as far the conditions for the payment are not at arm's length[19]. The same group of entities is defined as a direct or indirect interest of $1/3$[20]. A substantial interest exists if the shareholder holds at least 5% of the shares[21].

Furthermore, interest paid to an Exempt Company[22], in as far as the average loan of the Exempt Company to the debtor is more than 3 times the equity of the debtor. This rule also applies if the loan is granted by a foreign company that is not subject to tax on its profit. If the foreign company is subject to tax to its profit this rule does not apply and the interest is therefore deductible[23]

Financial criminal penalties imposed by a Curaçao criminal judge or amounts paid to avoid prosecution or financial penalties based on other Curaçao laws are not deductible from the profit[24]. A special limitation in the deduction of interest is stipulated in article 6A, paragraph 1 SOPT. Article 6A stipulates that the interest is not deductible if:

- The interest relates to a profit distribution or a repayment of capital by the tax payer;
- The interest relates to the acquisition of an interest of a group company as meant in article 1A, paragraph, letter a SOPT, established in one of the other countries

---

[18] Article 6 SOPT.
[19] Article 6 paragraph 2, letter c.
[20] Article 1A, paragraph 1, letter a.
[21] Article 11, paragraph 3 State Ordinance Income Tax.
[22] Article 1A, paragraph 1, letter f juncto paragraph 5.
[23] Article 6, paragraph 2, letter d.
[24] Article 6, paragraph 2, letter h.

of the Kingdom or a countries with which Curaçao has closed a treaty for the avoidance of double taxation, unless a change is established in the ultimate owner-ship or control in the acquired entity;

- The interest relates to a capital contribution or other form of equity contribution in the entity to which the loan is due.

Article 6A, paragraph 2, still allows deduction of inter-est in the situations, mentioned in article 6A, paragraph 1 SOPT in the following situation:

- The interest is based on mainly (in Dutch: "in overwe-gende mate") arm's length considerations;
- The interest is subject to a profit tax that is reasonable tax according to Curaçao standards.

Replacement reserve

If a an asset is sold, lost or damaged and the tax payer receives a payment in connection with this, the payment can be reserved and will not be added to the profit if the taxpayer has the intention to replace the sold, lost or dam-aged asset. The reserve will be added to the profit ultimately in the fourth financial year after the financial year in which the reserve was formed.

I.2.1.1.2.2. Taxpayers

Contrary to the BES-islands, Curaçao levies tax on profits of companies. Currently the profit tax rate is set at 22%[25]. Subject to tax in Curaçao are the legal entities which are mentioned in article 1, paragraph 1, letters a and b of the

---

[25] January 1, 2016

State Ordinance profit tax. Foundations and associations are only taxable if they are not only acting to satisfy public interests[26].

The foreign tax payers are mentioned in article 1, sub 1, paragraph c. Foreign tax payers are entities which are not established on Curaçao and (i) which have a permanent establishment on Curaçao, or (ii) which have real estate on Curaçao or rights related to real estate or (iii) have amounts receivable which – regarding the principle amount – are secured by mortgage on real estate in Curaçao[27] [28].

Whether an entity is established in Curaçao is determined based on circumstances. However, if the entity is governed by Curaçao law, then Curaçao is always considered as country of establishment[29].

I.2.1.1.2.3. Tax Rates

The profit tax rate is 22% as from January 1, 2016. Special minimum rates apply to the taxable income of certain companies. E-zone, new industries, hotels and land development companies fall under a rate of 2% for example.

I.2.1.1.3. Aruba

The corporate income tax rate of 25% is applicable to all business income that does not qualify for a special tax regime. Some types of activities are tax exempt or taxed at a lower rate than the general rate of 25%. In Aruba over the years many special tax regimes were introduced which were included in the existing corporate tax law. We will discuss this further below.

---

[26] Article 1, sub 1, paragraph b State Ordinance profit tax.
[27] Mr. J.P. Ruiter, AJV newsletter 2000, page 19 through page 26.
[28] Decisions Tax Appeal Court July 28, 2000, nrs. 1999/090 and 1999/091.
[29] Article 1, paragraph 2 SOPT.

I.2.1.1.3.1. Taxable event and taxable basis

Definition of profit

Article 3 of the State Ordinance Profit Tax describes the way the taxable profit of a company must be determined. CIT is levied according to the profit which is realized in the financial year of a company.

The profit which is realized in the financial year of the company is determined based on sound business practice (in Dutch: "goed koopmans gebruik"). According to article 3 the profit must be determined consistently, independent from the expected outcome (in Dutch: "bestendige gedragslijn"). The way the profit is determined ("tax accounting method") can only be changed if sound business practice justifies this. The tax authorities normally require as a condition for the change of the tax accounting method that no incidental fiscal advantage is realized. However, this is not a relevant condition. According to jurisprudence, the only relevant condition is whether an incidental fiscal advantage is intended[30].

In principle the financial year of the company is used for tax purposes. However, if the company does not maintain a regular bookkeeping with a yearly closing, the financial year is considered to be the calendar year.

Sound business practice is used for a proper allocation of the profit to the respective financial years of the company. Since sound business practice is not a clear and concrete definition of the way the yearly profit must be determined, in practice there can discussion about the explanation of sound business practice. Sound business practice is an old concept from Dutch tax law. Therefore there is a lot, old but also recent jurisprudence regarding the explanation of the concept of sound business practice. The concept of sound

---

[30] Vakstudie 16, Taxation of the Caribbean Kingdom Parts, note 7.2 to article 3 SOPT Aruba

business practice is still developing and changing, based on new insights, changes in accounting principles and introduction of new products and industries.

Starting point for the determination of the fiscal profit are the commercial financial statements. This was decided by the Dutch Supreme Court in 1957[31]. The Supreme Court decided that the commercial financial statement should be followed for the determination of the fiscal profit, unless application of tax law or general tax principles would lead to a difference between the commercial and fiscal profit. Although officially Dutch Supreme Court decisions regarding Dutch tax law have no relevance in Curaçao, in practice the Supreme Court decisions are followed.

Important tax principles which are used in sound business practice are:

- Matching principle (costs are allocated to the period in which the income is recognized)
- Reality principle (income and costs should be in accordance with the facts)
- Caution principle (unrealized profits are not taken into account, unrealized losses can – under certain conditions (brick judgment, see below) – be taken into account)
- Simplicity principle
- Consistency principle (a change of tax accounting principles is not allowed unless sound business practice allows the change[32])

An important decision regarding sound business practice is the decision of August 26, 1998[33] of the Dutch Supreme Court. Until that date a provision could only be formed if a legal obligation existed on balance date based on

---

[31] BNB 1957/208.
[32] Article 4, paragraph 5 SOPT
[33] BNB 1998/409

which the future payments should be made. The Supreme Court decided that this condition no longer applied but that a provision could be formed if the following three conditions were met:

- The provision is based on facts and circumstances which occurred before balance date
- The costs can be allocated to the period before balance date (matching principle)
- There is reasonable certainty that the costs will occur

Further definition of profit

In article 4 of the SOPT the so-called arm's length principle is defined. The arm's length principle means that related companies must deal with one another on a third party ("arm's length") basis. Therefore the related company must be seen as a third party for tax purposes for intercompany transactions. To apply the arm's length principle rules, first of all the related company must be defined. In the Aruba SOPT there are 2 definitions of a related company and the definitions are not the same. First of all a related company is defined in article 4 SOPT with respect to the arm's length principle. The second definition is stated in article 6 SOPT and relates to the limitation of the deduction of certain costs. We will first discuss the definition in article 4 SOPT

Related companies in article 4 SOPT

Article 4, paragraph 2 and 3 give a definition of a related company. This definition is very broad. If an entity, directly or indirectly, participates in the management or the supervision, or in the capital of another entity, the entities are considered as related entities for the application of the arm's length principle. Article 4, paragraph 2 broadens this definition by also including entities of which the same person, directly or indirectly, participates in the management or the supervision or the capital of one entity and another entity.

On Aruba it often happens that a person is a supervisory director of more than one company. These companies are considered related companies for the application of the arm's length principle. The consequence is that the conditions of article 4 SOPT regarding the arm's length principle have to be fulfilled. We will discuss these conditions below.

Conditions arm's length principle article 4 SOPT

If related parties, according to the above-mentioned definition, agree to conditions with respect to their intercompany transactions which deviate from conditions which independent third parties would have agreed to in normal economic dealings, the profit is determined according to conditions which independent third parties would have agreed to[34].

Furthermore, related entities must include documentation in their administration that demonstrates how the conditions of intercompany transactions are determined and why these conditions are at arm's length.

Treatment local shareholders of exempt companies[35]

If the shares of an exempt companies ex article 2, sub c SOPT are held by an entity as meant in article 1, paragraph 1, sub a and b, the not-distributed profits of an entity as meant in article 2, sub c SOPT. This means that if a local entity holds the shares of a tax exempted company, the exempted company will be considered to be transparent for tax purposes and the local shareholder will be taxed for the profits of the exempted company.

---

34 Article 4, paragraph 2 SOPT.
35 Referral is made to exempted companies as meant in article 2, sub c SOPT.

Liquidation, merger, demerger and transfer statutory seat[36]

In case of liquidation, merger, demerger and transfer of statutory seat of a company, then the increase of value of the assets which are transferred to the entitled entity is taxable. The transferred assets are set at the market value at the moment of transfer and the difference between the fiscal bookvalue and the market value is taxed.

In the reversed situation (assets become taxable in Aruba because of a merger or transfer of statutory seat to Aruba) a so-called step-up to the market value will be granted for these assets[37].

Deductible costs

Costs which have to be made to realize the profit can be deducted from the profit. Furthermore assets can be depreciated for tax purposes if the assets have a certain economic life. If after the economic life, the asset still has a residual value, this must be taken into account for the calculation of the depreciation. If the asset has a cost price of more than Awg 90,000,000, and the asset is used for an industrial company, the asset can be depreciated in 10 equal parts.

Investment allowance[38]

If an Aruban company invests more than Awg 5,000 in assets and these assets are purchased from an Aruban company, the investing company can claim an investment allowance of 6%. Investment allowance is a deduction on the taxable profit of a company. If – for example – a company invests for Awg 100,000 with another Aruban company, it can deduct 6% of Awg 100,000 is Awg 6,000 from its

---

[36] Article 4, paragraph 7 and 8 SOPT.
[37] Article 4, paragraph 9 SOPT.
[38] Article 5a SOPT.

taxable profit. So if the taxable profit before the investment allowance is Awg 20,000, after deduction of the investment allowance the taxable profit is Awg 14,000.

Certain items do not qualify for investment allowance, like ground and animals. A Free Zone company cannot apply the investment allowance.

Capital disposal charge[39]

If an asset is sold within 6 years after the investment allowance was claimed, a capital disposal charge must be paid on the selling price. The capital disposal charge is 6% on the selling price.

Limitation of deduction of costs[40]

Certain costs are not or not completely deductible from the taxable profit of a company. Monetary penalties, imposed by a criminal court and amounts paid to avoid criminal prosecution are not deductible. Furthermore administrative penalties, based on the General State Ordinance Taxes and State Ordinance purchase power compensation, are not deductible. Profit taxes on Aruba or a foreign country are not deductible from the profit. Neither are profit distributions.

Interest and other remunerations for the enjoyment of material or immaterial goods or rendered services, if due to entities, are not deductible, unless the tax payer makes credible that one of the following circumstances applies:

1. The interest or remunerations are not due to related persons or entities.
2. The interest or remunerations are subject to an effective tax rate of at least 15 percent.

---

[39] Article 5b SOPT.
[40] Article 6 SOPT.

3. The completely interest of the entity to which the interest or remunerations are due belongs to an entity of which, directly or indirectly, at least 50% of the shares, representing at least 50% of the voting rights, are registered at a qualifying Stock Exchange[41].

If the receiving entity does not pay an effective tax rate of at least 15% but can demonstrate that the receiving entity is subject to a taxation based on profit, 75% of the interest or remuneration can be deducted. In this respect it is important to demonstrate that there is indeed a taxation based on profit. If – for example – the receiving entity pays tax based on a cost-plus ruling, it might not be considered as a taxation based on profit[42].

Replacement reserve

If an asset is sold, lost or damaged and the tax payer receives a payment in connection with this, the payment can be reserved and will not be added to the profit if the taxpayer has the intention to replace the sold, lost or damaged asset. The reserve will be added to the profit ultimately in the fourth financial year after the financial year in which the reserve was formed.

1.2.1.1.2.2 Taxpayers

Contrary to the BES-islands, Aruba levies tax on profit of companies. Since January 1, 2016, the tax rate is 25% (it was 28% before January 1, 2016). Subject to tax in Aruba are the legal entities which are mentioned in article 1,

---

[41] Article 6, paragraph 3 SOPT.
[42] A cost-plus ruling calculates the taxable profit as a mark-up of a certain percentage of the costs.

paragraph 1 of the State Ordinance profit tax. Foundations and associations are only taxable if they are not only acting to satisfy public interests[43].

The foreign tax payers are mentioned in article 1, sub 1, paragraph c. Foreign tax payers are entities which are not established on Aruba and (i) which have a permanent establishment on Aruba, or (ii) which have real estate on Aruba or rights related to real estate or (iii) have amounts receivable which – regarding the principle amount – are secured by mortgage on real estate on Aruba[44] [45].

According to article 1, paragraph 2 in the following situations are in any case considered as a permanent establishment: (i) a permanent representative and (ii) a place of construction of a building or of construction-, digging-, maintenance, cleaning-, assembling or installation work if the duration is longer than 30 days.

If an entity is established in Aruba is determined based on circumstances. However, if the entity is governed by Aruban law, then Aruba is always considered as country of establishment[46].

1.2.1.1.2.3 Exemptions

Article 2 of the State Ordinance profit tax grants exemptions to 3 types of activities. The first category is a tax exemption for pension funds, savings funds, reservation funds, funeral funds, bad health funds and support funds for personnel or former personnel.

The second category is for entities of which the shares are held by Land Aruba and which activities consist of exploration and exploitation of oil.

---

[43] Article 1, sub 1, paragraph b State Ordinance profit tax.
[44] Mr. J.P. Ruiter, AJV newsletter 2000, page 19 through page 26.
[45] Decisions Tax Appeal Court July 28, 2000, nrs. 1999/090 and 1999/091.
[46] Article 1, paragraph 3 State Ordinance profit tax.

The third category are AVV's or VBA's which activities consist of activities which are mentioned in a State Decree[47].

1.2.1.1.2.4. Rate and refinery and terminal regime

The profit tax rate is 25%. For Free Zone companies the tax rate is 2%. Companies which operate an oil refinery or an oil terminal are subject to 12%. If this company is Stock Exchange listed, the tax rate is 7%. The oil refinery and terminal regime is also referred to as the OR/OT regime.

The minimum tax in the OR//OT regime is Awg 27,000,000. This amount will be increased yearly with an inflation correction. For the current owner of the refinery the minimum amount is Awg 18,000,000. If the tax paid according to the minimum amount due is higher than the tax due based on the percentage of the profit, the difference can be offset in the future if the actual tax is higher than the minimum amount.

I.2.2. Passive income

I.2.2.1. Curaçao

I.2.2.1.1. Dividends and capital gains

Participation exemption
Under the participation exemption regime, certain income such as dividends, stock dividends, bonus shares, hidden profit distributions and capital gains (including currency

---

[47] AB 2005/88: qualifying activities are (i) holding of shares and other participations, (ii) financing of other companies or entities, within or outside the own company, (iii) the investment of assets, except real estate, (iv) the licensing of industrial ownership rights and similar proprietary rights or rights of use according to the laws of Aruba and the laws of other countries.

gains) realized on the disposal of (part of) a qualifying interest in a Curaçao or foreign corporate entity are, in general, fully exempt from corporate income tax. Results derived from related currency hedge transactions are also exempted.

Costs which relate to a participation are not deductible, unless the costs contribute to profit, taxable in Curaçao. This also applies to transactions which are aimed to avoid currency risk with respect to a participation[48].

As a participation is considered:

- an ownership of at least 5% of the shares of the contributed capital or 5% of the voting rights of an entity of which the capital is divided in shares;
- membership of a cooperative;
- at least 5% of the participations of a fund that is appointed as a special fund as meant in article 1B, paragraph 1, or a comparable foreign special fund that is subject to tax.

As participation is also considered a related ownership of profit participations. If the participation is less than 5% as mentioned in article 11, paragraph 1, it is still deemed a participation if the cost price of the participation, together with the cost price of the shares which are already in the possession of the tax payer is at least Awg. 890,000.

Article 11, paragraph 4 SOPT gives a special regulation for so-called passive investments. Dividends from subsidiaries are only tax exempted for a part of 10/T (T is the tax rate) if:

- the gross revenue of the participation consists for more than 50% in dividend, interest or royalties, which are not received in the normal course of the business operation of the participation; and,

---

48 Article 11, paragraph 1 SOPT.

- the participation is not subject to a tax which is levied on the profit of the participation and which is at least 10% or which is subject to a foreign tax regime as mentioned in article 1A, paragraph 11[49].

This special regulation for passive investments does not apply to participations which assets consist, directly or indirectly, for 90% or more, of real estate.

Consolidated (group) financial statements can be used to substantiate the 2 requirements mentioned above (the type of income and the tax rate). The average of the relevant financial year and the 2 preceding financial years may be used for this purpose.

I.2.2.1.1.1. Taxable event
The taxable event is the realization of the participation income.

I.2.2.1.1.2. Taxable basis
The taxable basis is the dividend received or the capital gain realized with the disposal of the participation

I.2.2.1.1.3 Taxpayers
For taxpayers we refer to the tax subject as described above.

I.2.2.1.1.4 Tax rates
The income is not taken into account if the participation exemption applies. If the participation exemption does not apply, the normal tax rate of 22% applies to the income.

---

[49] According to article 1A, paragraph 11, foreign tax regime can be appointed as tax regimes which can be considered as similar to the Curaçao tax regime.

I.2.2.1.2. Interest

I.2.2.1.2.1. Taxable event
The taxable event is the realization of the interest income.

I.2.2.1.2.2. Taxable basis
The taxable basis is the interest received.

I.2.2.1.2.3. Taxpayers
For taxpayers we refer to the tax subject as described above.

I.2.2.1.2.4. Tax rates
The normal tax rate of 22% applies to the interest income, unless a special regime applies (see below).

I.2.2.1.3. Royalties

I.2.2.1.3.1. Taxable event
The taxable event is the realization of the royalty income.

I.2.2.1.3.2 Taxable basis
The taxable basis is the royalty received.

I.2.2.1.3.3. Taxpayers
For taxpayers we refer to the tax subject as described above.

I.2.2.1.3.4. Tax rates
The normal tax rate of 22% applies to the royalty income, unless a special regime applies (see below).

I.2.2.2. Aruba

I.2.2.2.1. Dividends and capital gains participation

Participation exemption

Income from participations is tax exempted. According to the law, income from participations is not taken into account (in Dutch: "blijft buiten aanmerking").

As a participation is a considered an ownership of shares or profit participations of an entity, association or foundation from businesses as mentioned in article 1, paragraph 1, letters a and b. Also a qualifying ownership of shares or profit participations in an entity which is not established in Aruba qualifies for the participation exemption.

A qualifying ownership is deemed to exist if the foreign participation is subject to tax on its profit and the shares are not held as a passive investment. The participation exemption does not apply to companies which are tax exempt based on article 2, letter c SOPT.

Costs which relate to a participation (for example interest costs) are not deductible in the first 2 years. The costs which have not been deducted in the first 2 years can be deducted in year 3, 4 and 5. As of year 3 the costs are normally deductible. Costs which are not deductible based on article 6, paragraph 2, letter f or article 6, paragraph 4 are not taxable[50].

I.2.2.2.1.1. Taxable event

The taxable event is the realization of the participation income.

---

[50] Article 11, paragraph 7 SOPT.

I.2.2.2.1.2. Taxable basis

The taxable basis is the dividend received or the capital gain realized with the disposal of the participation

I.2.2.2.1.3. Taxpayers

For taxpayers we refer to the tax subject as described above.

I.2.2.2.1.4. Tax rates

The income is not taken into account if the participation exemption applies. If the participation exemption does not apply, the normal tax rate of 25% applies to the income.

I.2.2.2.2. Interest

I.2.2.2.2.1. Taxable event

The taxable event is the realization of the interest income.

I.2.2.2.2.2. Taxable basis

The taxable basis is the interest received.

I.2.2.2.2.3. Taxpayers

For taxpayers we refer to the tax subject as described above.

I.2.2.2.2.4. Tax rates

The normal tax rate of 25% applies to the interest income, unless a special regime applies (see below).

I.2.2.2.3. Royalties

I.2.2.2.3.1. Taxable event
The taxable event is the realization of the royalty income.

I.2.2.2.3.2. Taxable basis
The taxable basis is the royalty received.

I.2.2.2.3.3. Taxpayers
For taxpayers we refer to the tax subject as described above.

I.2.2.2.3.4. Tax rates
The normal tax rate of 25% applies to the royalty income, unless a special regime applies (see below).

I.2.3. Special features of the CIT system

I.2.3.1. Curaçao

I.2.3.1.1. Existence of the Group Regime
It is possible to form a fiscal unity for profit tax purposes in Curaçao[51]. If a fiscal unity is formed, the parent company is assessed for the profit of the entities which form part of the fiscal unity. The parent company files a tax return for the consolidated profit of the entities which form part of the fiscal unity.

The most important conditions are:

---

[51] Article 14 SOPT and Ministerial Regulation Standard Conditions Fiscal Unity (P.B. 2002/151)

1. All the entities within the fiscal unity must have the same fiscal regime[52]. It is for example not possible to form a fiscal unity between an entity, which is subject to a tax rate of 2%, and an entity, which is subject to a tax rate of 22%.
2. Furthermore, the fiscal financial years of all the entities within the fiscal unity must be the same[53] and the parent entity must have at least 99% of the shares of the subsidiary[54].
3. The fiscal unity must be requested in the same financial year as the start of the fiscal unity[55].
4. Losses which are suffered before the start of the fiscal unity by one of the entities which form part of the fiscal unity can only be offset with the profits of this entity itself[56]. This is to avoid that entities with losses can be used to offset profits of profitable companies.

If at the moment the fiscal unity ends, losses are not offset yet, these losses remain with the parent company of the fiscal unity[57].

It is possible to use the fiscal unity and the participation exemption to avoid taxation on capital gains of assets. If, for example, a company wants sell an asset with a fiscal book-value of 100 and a market value of 200, it could transfer this asset to a newly incorporated entity within a fiscal unity. After that the shareholder could sell the shares of this newly incorporated entity, using the participation exemption. To avoid this, article 16 of the MB Standard Condition Fiscal Unity stipulates that if an asset is transferred to a subsidiary within a fiscal unity with a higher market value than fiscal

---

[52] Article 14, paragraph 3 SOPT.
[53] Article 14, paragraph 2 SOPT.
[54] Article 14, paragraph 1 SOPT juncto article 4 paragraph 1 Ministerial Decision Standard Conditions Fiscal Unity.
[55] Article 14, paragraph 1 SOPT.
[56] Article 11, paragraph 1 MB Standard conditions fiscal unity.
[57] Article 15, paragraph 10.

bookvalue at the moment of transfer the asset is set at the market value at the moment immediately preceding the end of the fiscal unity. If a replacement reserve is formed by the buyer of the asset, this replacement reserve is added to the profit at the moment immediately preceding the end of the fiscal unity[58].

This anti-abuse measure does not apply if:

- the transfer within fiscal unity took place under normal business circumstances;
- the transfer formed part of the transfer of a business or independent part of a business against the issuance of shares and after the moment of the transfer at least 3 financial years have lapsed;
- after the moment of transfer at least 6 financial years have lapsed.

I.2.3.1.2. Treatment of losses

Losses can be carried forward for 10 years after the year the loss is suffered. If a tax holiday industrial companies[59] or a tax holiday business establishment or hotel construction[60] suffers the losses in the first 4 years after the start of the tax holiday, the losses can be offset indefinitely.

I.2.3.1.3. Tax holidays

In Curaçao different kinds of tax holidays still apply[61]. At this moment the following tax holidays can be requested:

- a tax holiday incentives company establishment and hotel construction;
- a tax holiday ground development;

---

58 Article 16 MB Standard conditions fiscal unity.
59 P.B. 1985, no. 146.
60 P.B. 1953, no. 194.
61 In the BES islands and Aruba the tax holidays have been abolished.

- a tax holiday industrial companies;
- a tax holiday renovation hotels.

The tax holidays have different terms, different incentives and different objectives.

I.2.3.1.4. Insurance companies

A special regime exists for insurance companies in Curaçao[62]. Entities as mentioned in article 1, paragraph 1, letters a and b, which operate an insurance company, can request to determine the profit on 10% (life insurance) or 20% (other) of the received premiums and capital. For insurance coverage outside of Curaçao the percentages are 5%. This method is referred to as the premium method.

If an insurance company/entity elects the premium method, it must be elected together with the filing of the tax return and each time for a period of 5 years. If the insurance company/entity does not elect the premium method, the normal rules of sound business principles apply. An insurance company/permanent establishment can elect to report a pro rate part of the world wide profit of an insurance company. The pro rate part is calculated by dividing the premiums and capital received by the permanent establishment by the worldwide received premiums and capital by the insurance company. This fracture is multiplied by the worldwide profit of the insurance company. This last-mentioned profit is the profit that is considered to be the permanent establishment profit that can be allocated to Curaçao. The pro rate method can be elected in the tax return for consecutive periods of 5 years[63].

---

[62] Article 8 SOPT.
[63] Article 8, paragraph 5 SOPT.

I.2.3.1.5. Exempt Company[64]

An NV or BV in Curaçao can claim the tax exempt status. The NV or BV must file a written request with the tax inspector. The tax inspector must respond within 2 months on this request, otherwise it is considered to be granted[65]. The conditions to qualify for the exempt status are as follows:

- the management keeps a register of the names and addresses of the ultimate beneficial owners who have an interest of 10% or more in the entity;
- only natural persons, living in Curaçao, or certified trust offices, established in Curaçao, or the management of such trust offices or its employees form part of the management;
- the financial statements must be certified by a certified public accountant;
- the legal purpose and factual activities of the company are only or almost exclusively (i) lending of money, (ii) licensing of intellectual and industrial and similar proprietary or users rights according to the laws of Curaçao or the laws of other countries, passive investments in shares and deposits; and
- the company is not subject as a credit institution or other financial institution to supervision of the Bank of the Netherlands Antilles.

---

[64] Article 1A, paragraph 1, letter f.
[65] Article 1A, paragraph 2.

I.2.3.1.6. Export regime

As of January 1, 2014 the so-called export regime was introduced[66]. According to the export regime a tax rate of approximately 3.2%[67] applies to companies which gain 90% or more of their profits from goods sold or services rendered to international clients. The export regime serves as an alternative for the old offshore regime (subject to a tax rate of 2.4-3%) which is grandfathered through the 2019. The export regime is introduced for companies that act internationally. It allows the following activities:

- export of goods;
- international trade and services;
- repair and maintenance services performed on Curaçao to goods of foreign clients which will subsequently be returned abroad;
- repair and maintenance services performed abroad;
- international warehousing services;
- providing of loans and licenses, providing the use of intellectual property, acting as a holding company or being a member of a cooperation;
- other services performed for foreign clients.

Services which are excluded from the export regime are:

- acting as a director of companies whose registered office or effective management is situated in Curaçao and other similar trust services;
- services performed by a public notary, lawyers, accountants, tax advisers and other such services.

---

[66] Article 9 SOPT.
[67] Article 9, paragraph 1 SOPT stipulates that 95% of the profit is considered as foreign profit. This 95% is taxable against 10% of the normal tax rate as mentioned in article 15 SOPT.

I.2.3.1.7. Economic Zone

The E-zone is a designated area where goods can be stored, assembled, processed, packaged, displayed or handled in any other way. In Curaçao there are 2 E-zones for goods, one located at the airport, the other at the harbor. There are also E-zones where international trade and trade support-ive services can take place. This can be electronic commu-nication and information equipment (e-commerce). There are several e-commerce zones on Curaçao.

Financial services, royalty payments, insurance and reinsurance activities, trust services, services of civil-law notaries, lawyers, public accountants, tax counsellors and related services are not allowed in the E-zone.

The profit tax rate for E-zone companies is 2%. This rate does not apply to local sales or services on Curaçao. Furthermore, E-zone companies are not subject import duties, excise duties and turnover tax under certain con-ditions[68].

I.2.3.2. Aruba

I.2.3.2.1. Existence of a Group Regime

It is possible to form a fiscal unity for profit tax purposes on Aruba[69]. If a fiscal unity is formed, the parent company is assessed for the profit of the entities which form part of the fiscal unity. The parent company files a tax return for the consolidated profit of the entities which form part of the fiscal unity.

The conditions for the fiscal unity were published in 2006. There are 24 standard conditions for the fiscal unity. According to the fiscal unity conditions the parent com-pany is assessed for the consolidated profit of the fiscal unity entities. The parent company files a joint return for

---

[68] Article 9 State Ordinance Economic Zones 2000.
[69] Conditions Joint Venture 2006 (no date of publication).

all the fiscal unity entities[70]. Only Aruban NV's can form part of the fiscal unity[71]. The factual management of all the entities which form part of the fiscal unity must take place on Aruba.

All the entities within the fiscal unity must have the same fiscal regime. It is for example not possible to form a fiscal unity between an entity which is subject to a tax rate 10% and an entity which is subject to a tax rate of 25%. Furthermore, the fiscal financial years of all the entities within the fiscal unity must be the same and the parent entity must have at least 99% of the shares of the subsidiary[72].

The fiscal unity must be requested within 6 months after the start of the financial year. This request should include a so-called joint venture agreement, which forms the basis of the fiscal unity.

Losses which are suffered before the start of the fiscal unity by one of the entities which form part of the fiscal unity cannot be offset with profits of the fiscal unity[73]. This is to avoid that entities with losses can be used to offset profits of profitable companies. Normally in fiscal unity conditions it is possible to offset the losses with "own" profits of the entity with the carry forward losses. However, for simplicity sake, this is not possible on Aruba.

If at the moment the fiscal unity ends, losses are not offset yet, these losses remain with the parent company of the fiscal unity.

An anti-abuse regulation applies if the fiscal unity and the participation exemption are used to avoid taxation on capital gains of assets. If, for example, a company wants sell an asset with a fiscal book value of 100 and a market value of 200, it could transfer this asset to a newly incorporated entity within a fiscal unity.

---

[70] Standard condition 1.
[71] Standard condition 2. In practice Aruban VBA's are also allowed to form part of the fiscal unity.
[72] Standard condition 3, 4 and 5.
[73] Standard condition 11.

After that the shareholder could sell the shares of this newly incorporated entity, using the participation exemption. To avoid this, standard condition 18 stipulates that if:

- an asset or liability is transferred to a subsidiary within a fiscal unity, and
- the parent company has received a payment for the hidden reserves, including goodwill, by selling the shares in the subsidiary, and
- less than 6 book years have lapsed after the transfer of the asset or liability to the subsidiary.

The assets and liabilities are set at the market value at the end of the book year immediately preceding the split of the fiscal unity.

All the entities which form part of the fiscal unity are joint and several liable for taxes and premiums due by all the entities within the fiscal unity. After the end of the fiscal unity or after one of the entities leaves the fiscal unity, the liability remains in place for the period the entity was part of the fiscal unity[74].

Costs which relate to a participation of shares are not deductible[75]. This conditions relates to article 11, paragraph 6, SOPT. This limitation of deduction of costs is explicitly mentioned in the standard conditions, because it can be argued that within a fiscal unity the subsidiary does not "exist" anymore and therefore the costs are deductible.

However, at this moment the interest relating to a participation are deductible after 2 years (and the costs of year 1 and 2 in year 3, 4 and 5) according to article 11, paragraph 6 SOPT (for participations acquired in the financial year 2013 or later). This change in article 11 SOPT is not reflected yet in the fiscal unity conditions.

---

[74] Standard condition 20.
[75] Standard condition 21.

I.2.3.2.2. Treatment of Losses

Losses can be carried forward for 5 years after the year the loss is suffered. If a company applies the so called oil refinery and oil terminal regime[76], losses can be carried forward indefinitely.

I.2.3.2.3. Tax Holidays

Tax holidays have been abolished in Aruba as of January 1, 2003.

I.2.3.2.4. Insurance companies

A special regime exists for insurance companies in Aruba[77]. Entities as mentioned in article 1, paragraph 1, letters a and b, which operate an insurance company, can request to determine the profit on 10% (life insurance) or 20% (other) of the received premiums and capital. For insurance coverage outside of Aruba the percentages are 5% (life insurance) and 10% (other). This method is referred to as the premium method.

If an insurance company elects the premium method, it must be elected together with the filing of the tax return and each time for a period of 5 years. If the insurance company does not elect the premium method, the normal rules of sound business principles apply.

A permanent establishment must use the premium method, it does not have the possibility to use the normal use of sound business principles[78].

---

[76] Article 15, paragraph 6 through 12 SOPT.
[77] Article 8 SOPT
[78] In this respect referral is made to the decision of February 5, 2016, BBZ nr. 73890 of the Court in First Instance of Aruba.

I.2.3.2.5. 10% regime and hotel regime[79]

In Aruba certain companies can apply a different tax rate if these companies have a certain kind of activities. A tax rate of 10% applies for the following activities:

- Shipping and aviation
- Royalties
- Holding of shares and other participation rights
- Financing (not as credit institution)
- Passive investments
- Sustainable energy
- Agricultural, tuinbouw, fishing, imkerij, vee, of visteelt
- Scientific and cultural activities
- Medical tourism
- Rehabilitation for alcohol, drugs and other addiction
- Sustainable transportation with a low CO_2 emission
- Start up companies with respect to digitalizing company processes, 3D printing, Internet of Things, Big Data, robot- and nano technology and comparable start up companies

Hotel companies can apply a tax rate of 10%, 12% or 15%, depending on the Revenue per Available Room ("RevPar") of the hotel. The rate depends on the category which applies to the hotel. The following RevPar categories exist:

Category I: RevPar Afl 331 per day (excl. tourist levy) (CIT rate 10%).

Category II: RevPar Afl 313 per day (excl. tourist levy) (CIT rate 12%).

Category III: RevPar Afl 286 per day (excl. tourist levy) (CIT rate 15%).

Category IV: Diamond status (CIT rate 12%).

For each category investment requirements apply:

Category I: investment Afl 240K (more than 100 rooms); Afl 120K (100 rooms or less).

---

[79] Article 4 SOPT

Category II: investment Afl 165K (more than 100 rooms); Afl 75K (100 rooms or less).

Category III: investment Afl 90K (more than 100 rooms); Afl 45K (100 rooms or less).

Category IV: investment Afl 165K (more than 100 rooms); Afl 75K (100 rooms or less).

The investments have to be made as follows: 1/3 sustainability and environment, 1/3 training local employees, 1/3 locally produced products.

I.3. Corporate Income Tax on International Level

I.3.1. Tax Regulation for the Kingdom of the Netherlands ("BRK") and various bi-lateral agreements within the Kingdom of the Netherlands

I.3.1.1. Introduction

Tax matters within the Kingdom of the Netherlands used to be regulated by the BRK[80]. The BRK has many characteristics of a Tax Treaty to avoid double taxation between 2 countries. However, the BRK is a Kingdom law (in Dutch: "Rijkswet") which gives rules for (cross border) taxation of countries within the Kingdom of the Netherlands. As of the constitutional reform of the Kingdom on October 10, 2010, the BRK as such did not apply anymore since some islands became an independent country within the Kingdom (Curaçao and Sint Maarten; Aruba already had that status). The Netherlands and Aruba, Curaçao and Sint Maarten had the wish to conclude bi-lateral agreements regarding fiscal matters. The bi-lateral agreements are modeled after the OESO model treaty. However, certain specific matters are arranged differently in the bi-lateral

---

[80] Stb. 1964, 425, Kingdom Law of 28 October 1964

agreements. For example, the reduction of the dividend withholding tax to 0%, taxation of substantial interests, pensions, inheritance and gifts.

The bi-lateral arrangements have the advantage that no agreement is necessary between all countries within the Kingdom so that specific wishes and circumstances can be taken into account[81].

At this moment the bi-lateral agreements have been closed between The Netherlands and all the Dutch Caribbean islands[82] accept between The Netherlands and Aruba. Between the Dutch Caribbean islands itself no agreements have been closed yet. Based on the Kingdom Conference regarding Fiscal Affairs of 19 and 20 November 2009 in Aruba the BRK will remain applicable between the countries within the Kingdom that did not close a bi-lateral agreement[83].

The first regulation to take effect was the Tax Regulation Netherlands (in Dutch: "Belastingregeling Nederland")[84], which applied as of January 1, 2011, which applied between The Netherlands and the BES. After that Sint Maarten, Curaçao and Aruba negotiated their bi-lateral tax arrangements with The Netherlands, which resulted in bi-lateral agreements between The Netherlands and Sint Maarten and The Netherlands and Curaçao in 2015. Aruba stayed behind and does not have a bi-lateral tax agreement yet[85] with The Netherlands.

In general, the similarities and differences between the different tax regulations within the Kingdom of the Netherlands will be discussed. For each of the topics we will start

---

[81] WFR 2014/1437, De Belastingregeling voor Nederland en Curaçao, mr. A. Kattouw, mr. S. Vanenburg, prof. dr. R.P.W.C.M. Brandsma
[82] Agreements have been concluded between The Netherlands and Curaçao, The Netherlands and Sint Maarten and The Netherlands and the BES-islands.
[83] Kamerstukken II 2013/14, 33 955, nr. 3, p.1.
[84] Stb. 2011/107.
[85] In June 2016.

with the bi-lateral tax arrangements between The Netherlands and Curaçao[86] ("BNC") and The Netherlands and Sint Maarten[87] ("BNS") (which are almost similar).

These bi-lateral tax arrangements will be compared with the tax arrangement between The Netherlands and the BES-islands and the BRK (applicable between The Netherlands and Aruba, and Aruba, Curaçao and Sint Maarten).

I.3.1.2. Scope/area of application

BNC/BNS

The BNC and BNS only applies to taxation on income[88]. Residents of both countries can apply the treaty[89]. Natural persons who are residents of Curaçao and The Netherlands can apply the tie-breaker rule. In that case the usual rules of circumstances apply like center of (social) life, home, etc.

For entities the country of residence is the country where the entity is established according to the corporate income tax (The Netherlands) or profit tax (Curaçao), provided that the income of the entity is considered as income of the entity itself and not as income of its participants according to the legislation of The Netherlands or Curaçao[90] (for example the Private Foundation under certain conditions).

The BNC/BNS has a specific regulation for hybrid entities. A hybrid entity is an entity that is considered transparent for one country, but an entity for another country. This can cause double taxation or no taxation at all. If, for example, Curaçao considers an entity, established in Curaçao, as transparent and The Netherlands (place of

---

[86] Staatsblad 2015, nr. 348.
[87] Staatsblad 2016, nr. 21.
[88] Article 2, paragraph 1 BNC. Since article 28 BNC applies to inheritance and gift tax, this seems not completely correct.
[89] Article 1, paragraph 1 BNC.
[90] Article 4, paragraph 2 BNC

residence of the shareholders) considers this entity as non-transparent, income might not be taxable in either country (not in Curaçao because Curaçao does not recognize the entity and allocates the income to the shareholder and not in The Netherlands because The Netherlands assumes the income is taxable with the entity itself).

The hybrid entity rules in the BNC/BNS aim to avoid double taxation of income and no taxation of income. Both countries will consult each other in case of hybrid entities[91]. For certain specific situations a consultation is not necessary and the BNC/BNS will be applied[92].

BRK

In general the above-mentioned principles also apply to the BRK. The BRK does not have a regulation for hybrid entities.

BNB

In general the above-mentioned principles also apply to the BNB.

I.3.1.3. Dividend withholding tax

Based on article 10 BNC/BNA, the dividend withholding tax in the relation The Netherlands/Curaçao or Sint Maarten will not be levied in certain specific situations. If the conditions for the 0% rate are not met, the dividend withholding tax will be increased to 15%. Under a transitional regulation, the rate will be 5% through 2019, the year in which the offshore regime on Curaçao will expire[93].

---

[91] Article 4, paragraph 6 BNC
[92] Article 4, paragraph 7 BNC
[93] Article 30 BNC. This transitional regulation only applies if the entity was established in Curaçao on June 5, 2014.

To be eligible for the 0% rate for the dividend withholding tax, certain so-called limitation on benefits ("LOB") rules apply[94]. The LOB rules are similar to the Discussion Draft Action 6, based on the Action Plan on the Base Erosion and Profit Shifting of the OESO.

The 0% rate applies to pension funds and government entities[95]. Furthermore it applies for entities that hold at least 10% in an entity which is established in the dividend distributing country (in this case The Netherlands), provided that it meets one or more of the following conditions[96]:

- The entity is Stock Exchange listed at a qualifying Stock Exchange or the majority of the shares is held by a Stock Exchange listed entity [97];
- The entity is the head office of a multinational company[98];
- The entity employs at least 3 qualifying employees[99];
- The entity employs less than 3 qualifying employees but has real trading or business activities and the dividend relates to these trading or business activities[100];
- The entity has real business activities and less than 3 qualifying employees and the authorities of the distributing entities' country determine the incorporation, acquisition or maintenance of the entity does not have the purpose qualify for the benefits of the BNC/BNA[101] [102];
- The shares are for at least 50% held by a natural person, living in Curaçao or The Netherlands.

---

[94] Article 10, paragraph 4 BNC
[95] Article 10, paragraph 3, letters b and c BNC.
[96] Article 10, paragraph 3, letter a BNC.
[97] Article 10, paragraph 4, letter a BNC.
[98] Article 10, paragraph 4, letter b BNC.
[99] Article 10, paragraph 4, letter c BNC.
[100] Article 10, paragraph 5, letter a BNC.
[101] Article 10, paragraph 5, letter b BNC.
[102] Besluit van 14 juni 2014, Behandeling van verzoeken om zekerheid vooraf in de vorm van een Advance Tax Ruling (ATR), Stcrt. 2014, 15956.

Dividend distributions from the BES islands are always subject to 5% revenue tax.

BRK

Under the BRK, the dividend withholding tax was 8.3%, on dividends from The Netherlands to Curaçao with an interest of at least 25% of the contributed capital[103].

The Netherlands had the obligation to transfer the dividend withholding tax immediately to Curaçao after it had been withheld. For dividends from The Netherlands to Aruba the general rule applies (dividend withholding tax 7.5% or 5% with an interest of at least 25% of the contributed capital)[104].

Since the BNC and BNS have been introduced, the BRK does not apply anymore on dividends from The Netherlands to Curaçao and Sint Maarten. However, the BRK still applies between The Netherlands and Aruba.

Curaçao itself does not levy a dividend withholding tax, so no dividend withholding tax is due on dividends from Curaçao to The Netherlands.

BNB

According to the BNB, dividends paid are taxable in the country of residence of the shareholder. The country of residence of the distributing entity is also entitled to levy tax on the dividend according to its domestic tax rules[105].

However, if the ultimate shareholder is established in the BES islands and has an interest of at least 10% of the shares of the distributing entity in The Netherlands, the dividends are not taxable in The Netherlands.

---

[103] Article 11, paragraph 3, letter a BRK.
[104] Article 11, paragraph 3 BRK.
[105] Article 2.4, paragraph 2 BNB.

I.3.1.4. Pensions and annuities

BNC/BNS

According to the BNC/BNS, the taxation rights on pensions are divided between the source state and the country of residence. Normally, cross border situations, pensions are taxable in the country of residence, except in case of surrender of pensions and government pensions. The BNC/BNS determines that in case of private pensions, the source country has the right to tax to a maximum of 15% on pensions[106]. The country of residence also has the right to levy tax on pensions, however, the tax levied by the source state must be offset against the tax levied by the country of residence. Surrender of a pension remains taxable in the source state and government pensions remain taxable in the source country. The afore-mentioned rules are also applicable to annuities which are fiscally facilitated[107].

BRK

According to the BRK pensions are taxable in the country of residence of the person who enjoys the pension[108]. If the pension is surrendered, transferred or the pension is enjoyed in another manner, than the pension is also taxable in the country in which the pension was built up in the past[109]. This last-mentioned rule also applies to government pensions[110]. The taxation of pensions under the BRK and under the BNC has been changed in the sense that under the BNC also the country from which the pension is paid can levy a tax of up to 15% in case of an annuity. This was not possible under the BRK.

---

[106] Article 17, paragraph 3 BNC.
[107] Article 18, paragraph 4 BNC.
[108] Article 15, paragraph 4 BRK.
[109] Article 15, paragraph 6 BRK.
[110] Article 17 BRK.

BNB

According to the BNB pensions are taxable in the country of residence of the persons who enjoys the pensions[111]. If the pension is surrendered before the date the pension would start, the pension is also taxable in the country in which the pension was built up in the past[112].

The last-mentioned rule also applies to government pensions[113]. Therefore the BNB still follows the BRK with respect to pensions.

I.3.1.5. Inheritance and gifts

BNC/BNS

Under the BNC/BNA this term is extended to 5 years in case of gifts and death.

BRK

Under application of the BRK rules, the gift tax can "follow" an emigrated person for 1 year. With other words, if a gift is done within 12 months after emigration, the former country of residence still has the right to levy an additional amount of gift tax (on top of what was already levied by the country of residence). The total amount of gift tax cannot exceed the amount that would have been levied by both countries together, if the emigration would not have taken place.

In case of death, the right to levy inheritance tax goes to the country of residence on the first day after the emigration[114].

---

[111] Article 2.9, paragraph 1 BNB.
[112] Article 2.9, paragraph 2 BNB.
[113] Article 2.10 BNB.
[114] Article 29 BRK.

BNB

The BNB does not apply to inheritance and gift tax.

I.3.1.6. Anti-abuse

According to the BNC/BNA[115] the countries can apply its domestic regulations in case of fraud or abuse.

I.3.1.7. Tax treaties in force

General

Curaçao currently has tax treaties in effect with Aruba (BRK), the Netherlands (BNC), Norway, St. Maarten (BRK) and Jamaica.

The Dutch Caribbean islands mostly have Tax Information Exchange Agreements (TIEA's). TIEA's have been signed by Curaçao with several countries, including Australia, Canada, Colombia, Denmark, Mexico, New Zealand, Spain, Sweden, and the United States. In the Global Forum on Transparency and Exchange of Information for Tax Purposes Peer Reviews 2015: Curaçao 2015 (phase 2: Implementation of the Standard in Practice) of the OECD, Curaçao has been rated as partially compliant. Following the phase 1 Curaçao made significant improvements to its legal framework, which ensures the availability, access and exchange of information. However, according to the review there was a lack of oversight and enforcement of this legal framework.

Please note that the tax treaties of The Netherlands do not apply to Aruba, Curaçao and Sint Maarten. However, tax treaties which are closed after the constitutional reform of the Kingdom in 2010 can apply to the BES

---

[115] Article 22 BNC/BNA.

islands. According to the Dutch Treaty policy, The Netherlands include the European part of The Netherland and the BES islands Bonaire, Sint Eustatius and Saba[116].

In the Tax Treaty between The Netherlands and China the BES islands are – for example – explicitly mentioned in article 3, paragraph 1, letter b, under (ii). Curaçao signed an IGA ("Intergovernmental agreement") with the United States on 16 December 2014. Financial institutions in Curaçao must file the required reporting with regard to the Foreign Account Tax Compliance Act (FATCA) through a website set up by the Curaçao government.

I.4. Anti-Avoidance Legislation

I.4.1. Abuse of law

I.4.1.1.BES islands

The BES islands do not have specific anti-abuse regulations.

I.4.1.2. Curaçao

Curaçao does not have specific anti-abuse regulations.

I.4.1.3. Aruba

Aruba does not have specific anti-abuse regulations.

I.4.2. Thin capitalization rules

I.4.2.1. BES islands

No thin capitalization rules exist in the BES islands.

---

[116] WFR 2013/1474, Het nieuwe belastingverdrag met China: "Black cat or white cat: If it can catch mice, it's a good cat!", Mr. J. Adeler.

I.4.2.2. Curaçao

No thin capitalization rules exist in Curaçao. The limitation in the deduction of certain costs can work as a thin capitalization in some circumstances. We refer to the chapter regarding the limitation in deduction of costs in Curaçao.

I.4.2.3. Aruba

No thin capitalization rules exist in Aruba.

I.4.3. CFC legislation

I.4.3.1. BES islands

No CFC legislation exists in the BES-islands.

I.4.3.2. Curaçao

No CFC legislation exists in Curaçao.

I.4.3.3. Aruba

No CFC legislation exists in Aruba.

I.5. Tax treaty law

I.5.1. BES islands

No specific tax treaty law exists in the BES-islands. Since The Netherlands include the BES islands in their most recent tax treaties, the tax treaties law of The Netherlands applies to the tax treaties of the BES islands.

I.5.2. Curaçao

No specific tax treaty law exists in Curaçao.

I.5.3. Aruba

No specific tax treaty law exists in Aruba.

I.5.1. Adherence to UN or OECD Model Tax Convention

I.5.1.1. BES islands

Since The Netherlands include the BES islands in their most recent tax treaties, the general adherence to the OECD Model Tax Convention applies to the tax treaties of the BES islands.

I.5.1.2. Curaçao

Since Curaçao does not have any recent tax treaties, this question does not apply to Curaçao. The bi-lateral agreements between the islands and with The Netherlands are modeled after the OECD Model Tax Convention.

I.5.1.3. Aruba

Since Curaçao does not have any recent tax treaties, this question does not apply to Curaçao. The bi-lateral agreements between the islands and with The Netherlands are modeled after the OECD Model Tax Convention.

I.5.2. Special Features commonly present in Tax Treaties

1.5.2.1.BES islands

Since The Netherlands include the BES islands in their most recent tax treaties, the treaty policy of The Netherlands applies to the tax treaties of the BES islands.

I.5.2.2. Curaçao

Since Curaçao does not have any recent tax treaties, this question does not apply to Curaçao.

I.5.2.3. Aruba

Since Curaçao does not have any recent tax treaties, this question does not apply to Curaçao.

I.5.3. Treaties currently in force

I.5.3.1.BES islands

The tax treaties of The Netherlands do not apply to Aruba, Curaçao and Sint Maarten. However, tax treaties which are closed after the constitutional reform of the Kingdom can apply to the BES islands. According to the Dutch Treaty policy, The Netherlands include the European part of The Netherlands and the BES islands Bonaire, Sint Eustatius and Saba[117]. In the Tax Treaty between The Netherlands and China the BES islands are – for example – explicitly mentioned in article 3, paragraph 1, letter b, under (ii).

I.5.3.2. Curaçao

Curaçao currently has tax treaties in effect with Aruba, the Netherlands, Norway and St. Maarten.

I.5.3.3. Aruba

Aruba currently has tax treaties in effect with Curaçao, the Netherlands and St. Maarten.

---

[117] WFR 2013/1474, Het nieuwe belastingverdrag met China: "Black cat or white cat: If it can catch mice, it's a good cat!", Mr. J. Adeler.

1.6. Community law

I.6.1. Participation in a Community/Union

I.6.1.1.BES islands

The BES islands form part of the (European) Netherlands as special municipalities. The BES islands are so-called public entities as referred to in article 134 of the Dutch Constitution. The Netherlands are a EU member state. Although the BES islands are part of the Netherlands as special municipalities, the BES-islands maintained their status as Overseas Territory[118].

I.6.1.2. Curaçao

Curaçao has the status of Overseas Territory of a member state of the European Union.

I.6.1.3. Aruba

Aruba has the status of Overseas Territory of a member state of the European Union.

---

[118] Decision 2013/755/EU of the Council of 25 November 2013 regarding the association of overseas territories with the European Union.

3

Brazil

Dr. Fernando Souza de Man

I. Introduction

The Brazilian Tax system is extremely complex, and compliance to the rules demands significant work. As a matter of fact, according to the study *Paying Taxes 2017*[1], conducted by the World Bank and PwC, a medium sized company spends 2.038 hours per year to pay taxes in Brazil[2], which is almost twice as many hours needed in Bolivia, second in the rank, and much higher than the Latin American countries average, which is 564 hours. Furthermore, Brazil is ranked at 181 out of 189 economies on the easiness of paying taxes.

Taking this complexity in consideration, as well as the international perspective of this course, this chapter will not discuss in detail all taxes to which a corporation is subject to in Brazil; it will rather focus on the corporate income tax, providing its main characteristics and discussing its application in domestic and international situations. Further, this contribution will deal with the domestic legis-

---

[1] Paying Taxes 2017, World Bank Group & PwC, available at https://www.pwc.com/gx/en/paying-taxes/pdf/pwc-paying-taxes-2017.pdf, p. 124, last accessed on 14 July 2017. This is a considerable reduction from the previous year, in which companies needed 2600 hours to comply with their obligations, but Brazil is still the outright leader in this regard.

[2] *Paying Taxes 2017*, (note 165), p. 124.

lation devised to counter tax avoidance schemes and the double tax conventions signed by Brazil, as well as recent amendments influenced by the OECD work on BEPS.

I.1 Corporate Income Tax at Domestic Level

The Brazilian system of income taxation, including the taxation of corporate entities, is structured according to the principles established in the Brazilian Constitution [3], the National Tax Code [4], the Income Tax Regulation, issued in 1999 ("ITR/99") [5], and subsequent laws (complementary and ordinary), decrees and provisional measures edited by the Government.

On that matter, the Brazilian Constitution stipulates that income taxes shall be levied by the Federal Government and that they should be general (all income earned), universal (all income-earners) and progressive (higher earners should pay more), in accordance with the law[6], while the National Tax Code determines that taxes shall be levied on earnings from capital, labor (or a combination of both) and any increase in wealth [7].To facilitate our study, income will be divided into active and passive income

---

[3]   Brazil, Constitution of the Federal Republic of Brazil, 1998, available at http://www.planalto.gov.br/ccivil_03/constituicao/ConstituicaoCompilado.htm, last accessed on 15 July 2017.

[4]   Brazil, National Tax Code (Law n. 5172/66), available at http://www.planalto.gov.br/ccivil_03/leis/L5172Compilado.htm, last accessed on 15 July 2017.

[5]   Brazil, Income Tax Regulation (Decree n. 3000/99), available at http://www.planalto.gov.br/ccivil_03/decreto/d3000.htm, last accessed on 20 July 2017.

[6]   Brazil, Constitution of the Federal Republic of Brazil, 1998,(note 167), art. 153.

[7]   Brazil, National Tax Code (note 168), Article 43.

I.1.1. Active Income

Active income is the income derived from the exercise of an activity, either through employment or, in the case of companies, of business[8].

I.1.1.1. Business Profits

The Taxation of Business Profits is regulated by Book II of the ITR/99, where it is prescribed the taxable event, basis, immunities as well as rules for small and medium enterprises.

I.1.1.1.1. Taxable Event

According to Article 43 of the National Tax Code, mentioned afore, there is no question that the taxable event for the corporate income tax is the earning of income, whether through labor, capital, or a combination of both, or the increase in wealth. Article 218 of the ITR/99 confirms this approach, stating that corporate income tax is due whenever income is earned[9].

I.1.1.1.2. Taxable Basis

The taxable base can be asserted mainly in two manners, by a real profit regime or a presumed profit regime[10]. The real profit regime is obligatory for some taxpayers, e.g. enterprises that earned more than 78 million reais in the previous year or earned income abroad[11], and in this case

---

8   IBFD Tax Glossary, available at www.ibfd.org, last accessed on 17 July 2017.
9   Brazil, Income Tax Regulation (note 169), art. 218.
10 In specific cases, the tax authorities can arbitrage the profits which are subject to tax, but as these situations are limited they will not be discussed in this work. Also, Brazil prescribes a special, simpler regime for small and medium enterprises.
11 Brazil, Ordinary Law n. 9.718/98, available at http://www.planalto.gov.br/ccivil_03/LEIS/L9718.htm#art14, article 14, last accessed on 18 July 2017.

the taxpayer effectively calculates the profits achieved in the year, considering all income earned in the period, with the additions and exclusions authorized in the Regulation[12]. On that matter, expenses which are necessary for the development of the activity are generally deductible[13], although some restrictions may exist.

On the other hand, enterprises that earned less than 78 million reais in the previous fiscal year and are not obliged by law to adopt the real profit regime can adopt a system of presumptive taxation, the presumed profit regime. In this regime, the taxable basis is determined by the assumption that the enterprise, depending on its activity, earned a profit ranging from 1,6% (sale of fuel and natural gas) to 32% (services in general) of its gross revenue.

As the profit margin is based on a presumption, the taxpayer cannot deduct any expense related to the earning of the income. Furthermore, income not related to the income-earning activity of the taxpayer, e.g. capital gains, interest, is not subject to the presumed profit margin; such income should be added to the result of the presumed profit and subject to the corresponding tax rates. In this regime, after the gross revenue is multiplied by the presumed profit margin, the result still must be subject to the tax rates for corporate income tax to determine the tax due.

I.1.1.1.3. Taxpayers

Concerning the taxpayer, as expressed at ITR/99, the corporate income tax is due by legal persons[14], which are defined as: (i) legal persons domiciled in Brazil[15]; and (ii) branches, agencies and representative offices of legal persons resident abroad[16]. The definition of corporate domi-

---

12 Brazil, Income Tax Regulation (note 169), Art. 247.
13 Brazil, Income Tax Regulation (note 169), Art. 299.
14 Brazil, Income Tax Regulation (note 169), Article 146, I.
15 Brazil, Income Tax Regulation (note 169), Article 147, I.
16 Brazil, Income Tax Regulation (note 169), Article 147, II.

cile is provided on ITR/99, which states that the company is domiciled at its headquarters or, in case of a PE or representation of a foreign enterprise, the place where such PE or representation is located[17].

Furthermore, the ITR/99 determines that silent partnerships shall be treated in the same manner as legal persons[18]. Thus, in the Brazilian legislation unincorporated entities are subject to corporate income tax. Also, the regulation prescribes that foreign enterprises deriving income sourced in Brazil shall be taxed therein[19].

I.1.1.1.4. Tax rates

In Brazil, there are two applicable tax rates for the corporate income tax, a 15% general tax[20] and a surtax of 10% on the amount that exceeds 20.000 reais in a month[21].

Furthermore, there is no withholding tax obligation if the business activity developed by the taxpayer amounts to the sale of goods, save in case the payment was made by an entity of the public administration to a private legal entity. However, in case of the provision of services by legal entities to legal entities or the government, the payer of the services legal entity is obliged to withhold part of the tax, with rates varying in accordance with the service provided[22].

I.1.2. Passive Income

Passive income is the income derived from the holding of assets[23], e.g. dividends, interest and royalties.

---

17 Brazil, Income Tax Regulation (note 169), Article 212.
18 Brazil, Income Tax Regulation (note 169), Article 148.
19 Brazil, Income Tax Regulation (note 169), Article 685.
20 Brazil, Income Tax Regulation (note 169), 541.
21 Brazil, Income Tax Regulation (note 169), 542.
22 Brazil, Income Tax Regulation (note 169), Arts. 647-653.
23 IBFD Tax Glossary, available at www.ibfd.org, last accessed on 17 July 2017.

I.1.2.1. Dividends

Since 1996, Brazil does not tax dividends paid by its resident companies to residents and non-residents[24].

I.1.2.2. Interest

I.1.2.2.1. Taxable Event

Like the case of business profits, the taxable event is the earning of interest income[25].

I.1.2.2.2. Taxable Basis

The taxable base is, at first, the amount of interest earned, which is subject to a withholding tax at the moment of payment. Afterwards, this income shall be added to the income from business activities when calculating the profits earned by the legal entity[26]. Costs linked to the earning of the interest income are deductible, if they comply with the requirements of being usual and necessary for the earning of the income[27].

I.1.2.2.3. Taxpayers

The tax is due by the legal entity that received the interest payment, i.e. the one that lent the money[28].

---

[24] Brazil, Ordinary Law n. 9,249/95, article 10, available at http://www.planalto.gov.br/ccivil_03/LEIS/L9249.htm#art10, last accessed on 17 July 2017.

[25] Brazil, Income Tax Regulation (note 169), art. 373.

[26] Brazil, Income Tax Regulation (note 169), art. 373.

[27] Brazil, Income Tax Regulation (note 169), Art. 299.

[28] Brazil, Income Tax Regulation (note 169), art. 373.

I.1.2.2.4. Tax rates

Interest income earned by legal entities is subject to a with-holding tax that varies from 15% up to 22.5%, depending on the due date of the payment (interest earned on loans for less than 180 days are subject to the 22.5% tax rate while loan with a maturity date longer than 720 days are subject to the 15% tax rate[29].

Furthermore, this amount will be added to profits of the enterprise, and will then be subject to the 15% general tax rate[30] and a surtax of 10% on the amount that exceeds 20.000 reais in a month[31].

I.1.2.3. Royalties

I.1.2.3.1. Taxable Event

The receipt of royalty payments, as it represents and increase on the wealth of the taxpayer, is the taxable event[32].

I.1.2.3.2. Taxable Basis

The taxable base is the value paid as royalty subtracted from the expenses needed for the maintenance and fruition of the asset that entitles the entity to the royalty payments[33]. On that matter, royalties paid to shareholders, managers and their family members are not considered necessary expenses, so they are non-deductible[34]

---

[29] Brazil, Ordinary Law n. 11.033/04, Art. 1, available at www.planalto.gov.br, last accessed on 21 July 2017. Loans with maturity dates from 181 up to 360 days are subject to a 20% rate while loans from 361 up to 720 days are subject to a 17.5% tax rate.
[30] Brazil, National Tax Code (note 168), 541.
[31] Brazil, Income Tax Regulation (note 169), 542.
[32] Brazil, Income Tax Regulation (note 169), art. 373.
[33] Brazil, Income Tax Regulation (note 169), art. 352.
[34] Brazil, Income Tax Regulation (note 169), Art. 353, I.

I.1.2.3.3. Taxpayers

The tax is due by the legal entity that received the royalty payment, i.e. the one that owns the intellectual property[35].

I.1.2.3.4. Tax rates

Royalty income falls under the general rates of taxation, i.e. 15%[36] and a surtax of 10% on the amount that exceeds 20.000 reais in a month[37]. In case of royalty payments made between corporate entities there is no withholding obligation.

I.1.3. Special Features of the Corporate Income Tax System

While this work has focused on the corporate income tax, it should be borne in mind that Brazil also has a social contribution on net profit, whose proceeds are earmarked for the financing of the social security system, which resembles the corporate income tax. As a matter of fact, the corporate income tax and the social contribution on net profit have similar tax bases and taxpayers (legal persons domiciled in Brazil). Regarding its tax rate, this contribution is levied at the general rate of 9%, with specific rates for certain fields of activity, e.g. banks are subject to a 20% rate[38].

Also, in the presumed profit regime the profit margins are set at 12% for commercial activities and 32% for services in general. Given its similarity to the corporate income tax, it is common in Brazil to say that the corporation is subject to a tax of 34% (15% of the corporate income tax, 10% of the surtax, and 9% of the social contribution).

---

35 Brazil, Income Tax Regulation (note 169), art. 373.
36 Brazil, Income Tax Regulation (note 169), 541.
37 Brazil, Income Tax Regulation (note 169), 542.
38 Brazil, Ordinary Law n. 7.689/89, available at www.planalto.gov.br, last accessed on 21 June 2016.

At last, notwithstanding the non-taxation of dividends, there is a system of interest on net equity in which part of the amount distributed to the shareholders, subject to the same requirements as the distribution of dividends, can be deducted from the corporate income tax base while the receipt of this income is taxed at a 15% rate[39]

I.1.3.1. Group Regime

Brazil has no special group regime for corporations when acting strictly in its territory, as tax consolidation is not allowed and companies are always taxed as independent enterprises.

I.1.3.2. Treatment of losses

There is no limitation for the carrying-forward of losses, but they cannot be used to offset more than 30% of the income tax due in a year[40]. Furthermore, there is no carry-back of losses.

I.1.3.3. Tax Holidays

Brazil gives regional incentives for countries to invest is specific regions of the country, such as the north and north-east regions, and in specific fields, such as R&D expenses.

I.2 Corporate Income Tax on International Level

As studied in the previous section, in fully domestic situations Brazil levies corporate income tax on all income (save dividend income) earned by enterprises domiciled in the country, irrespective of whether they are incorporated, and taxation is based on an actual profit or presumed profit regime, with a general tax rate of 15% and a surtax

---

[39] Brazil, Income Tax Regulation (note 169), Art. 347.
[40] Brazil, Income Tax Regulation (note 169), Art. 250.

of 10% on the actual or presumed profit earned. In this section we will focus on taxation of income in inbound and outbound situations, i.e. when income is earned by a Brazilian company abroad or when a foreign enterprise earns income in Brazil.

Before proceeding it is important to bear in mind that there is no domestic definition of PE in the Brazilian legislation and, as mentioned afore, for income tax purposes these establishments are treated as resident companies, being also liable for paying the tax.

I.2.1. Inbound transactions

For matters of practicality, this session will be divided in the same topics as the previous.

I.2.1.1. Active Income

For the definition of active income, refer to section I.1.1.

I.2.1.1.1. Business Profits

Business profits of non-resident enterprises are also subject to taxation in Brazil.

I.2.1.1.1.1 Taxable Event

The earning of income in Brazil is the link for taxation of foreign entities in Brazil.

I.2.1.1.1.2. Taxable Basis

The tax base varies depending on whether business is conducted through a permanent establishment or not. If there is a permanent establishment, profits earned by this entity will be treated just like profits of a resident, being subject to the actual profit regime or the presumed profit regime

I.2.1.1.1.3. Taxpayers
The taxpayer will be the non-resident entity itself or, in case there is a permanent establishment in Brazil, the permanent establishment.

I.2.1.1.1.4. Tax rates
The tax rates depend on whether business is conducted through a permanent establishment or not. In case there is a permanent establishment in Brazil, it will be the 15% corporate income tax. Potentially the 10% surtax, as well as 9% on the social contribution on net profits. On the other hand, if the non-resident does not have a permanent establishment in Brazil, the tax will be withheld at source, normally at the general rate of 15% of the gross revenue[41]. In case of the provision of services (except services of a technical nature, which are also subject to a 15% tax rate) or employment income, however, the rate is increased to 25%[42]

I.2.1.2. Passive Income

I.2.1.2.1. Dividends
Dividends paid by Brazilian companies to foreign investors are not subject to taxation, i.e. the treatment is the same given to Brazilian residents.

I.2.1.2.2. Interest
Just like dividend payments made between residents, payments made to non-residents are also subject to taxation.

---

[41] Brazil, Income Tax Regulation (note 169), Art. 685.
[42] Brazil, Income Tax Regulation (note 169), Art. 685, II.

I.2.1.2.2.1 Taxable Event

The taxable event is the payment of interest to the non-resident.

I.2.1.2.2.2. Taxable Basis

The basis, in the case of the presence of a permanent establishment, is the income earned after the deduction of the costs attached to this interest. If there is no permanent establishment in Brazil, the tax base is the gross interest revenue.

I.2.1.2.2.3. Taxpayers

The non-resident earning the income.

I.2.1.2.2.4. Tax rates

In case a permanent establishment exists, rates are the same as applied domestically. As for payments made directly to the non-resident entity, there will be a withholding tax of 15%[43].

I.2.1.2.3. Royalties

Royalties earned by non-residents is also subject to taxation in Brazil.

I.2.1.2.3.1. Taxable Event

The payment of royalties by a Brazilian resident to a non-resident.

---

[43] Brazil, Income Tax Regulation, (note 169), article 702

I.2.1.2.3.2. Taxable Basis

If there is a permanent establishment in Brazil, the rules are the same applicable to resident entities. But if there is no permanent establishment, there will be a tax on the gross royalty payment.

I.2.1.2.3.3. Taxpayers

The non-resident royalty recipient.

I.2.1.2.3.4. Tax rates

In case a permanent establishment exists, rates are the same as applied domestically. As for payments made directly to the non-resident entity, there will be a withholding tax of 15%[44].

I.2.1.3. Special Features of the CIT system

I.2.1.3.1. Existence of Group Regime

Just like domestically, there is no group regime involving non-residents.

I.2.1.3.2. Treatment of Losses

If losses are made through a permanent establishment, they are subject to the same rules as domestic enterprises. Otherwise, since taxation occurs on gross income, there is no right to the consideration of losses.

---

[44] Brazil, Income Tax Regulation, (note 169), article 702

I.2.1.3.3. Tax Holidays

There are special provisions for investments in government bonds, but no general tax holidays regarding specifically non-resident enterprises.

I.2.1.3.4. Relations with Tax Havens or Low Tax Regimes

Although, as a rule, income paid to foreign entities is subject to a 15% final withholding tax, the Brazilian law prescribes that whenever a payment is made to a resident of a low tax jurisdiction, the withholding tax shall be charged at the rate of 25% [45]. For that matter, low tax jurisdiction is defined as a jurisdiction which does not charge income tax or charges at a rate lower than 20% [46] or which does not provide information on the ownership of shares of a legal entity and on the beneficial owner of income attributed to non-residents[47].

More recently the concept of fiscal privileged regime was also introduced in the Brazilian legal system. A fiscal privileged exists whenever any of the following characteristics is present: (i) income, domestic or international, is not taxed or taxed at a rate lower than 20%[48]; (ii) a tax benefit is granted to no)n-residents in the absence of substantial economic activity in the country or conditioned to the absence of such substantial activity; and (iii) the country does not provide information on the ownership of shares of a legal entity and on the beneficial owner of income attributed to non-residents[49].

---

[45] Brazil, Ordinary Law n. 9.779/99, available at www.planalto.gov.br, last accessed on 22 June 2016, Art. 8.

[46] Brazil, Ordinary Law 9.430/96, available at www.planalto.gov.br, last accessed on 22 June 2016, Art. 24. This percentage has been reduced to 17% in case of countries which signed an agreement with Brazil containing a clause on exchange of information or are committed to standards set by international organizations as the Global Forum on Tax Transparency and Exchange of Information

[47] Brazil, (note 210), Art. 24, paragraph 4.

[48] This amount has been reduced to 17%. See note 210.

[49] Brazil, (note 210), Art. 24-A.

Diverging from the situation concerning low-tax jurisdictions, in the case of payments made to entities benefitting from fiscal privileged regime there is no increase on the Brazilian WHT tax, i.e. income will be taxed at the rate of 15%, as the law prescribing the increase on the rate makes expressly reference only to situations involving low tax jurisdictions[50].

This is the sole major difference in treatment between payments made to entities resident in low tax jurisdictions and benefitting from a fiscal privileged regime, since in both cases the Brazilian: (i) transfer pricing rules will be applicable, even if the parties are not related[51]; (ii) thin cap rules will be more stringent than in case of payments made to entities not located on low-tax jurisdictions or benefitting from fiscal privileged regimes [52]; and (iii) payments made to the foreign entity will only be deducted from the corporate income tax base if the following requirements are cumulatively met: (a) the beneficial owner of the income is disclosed to the tax authorities; (b) it is proved that this foreign entity carries out the activity for which it is being paid; and (c) the Brazilian entity provides documental evidence confirming the actual payment and the receipt of goods of services[53].

I.2.2. Outbound Transactions

Brazilian residents are subject to the corporate income tax on a worldwide basis, i.e. income earned abroad is also subject to income tax in Brazil[54]. Consequently, Brazil will provide a credit for taxes paid abroad to avoid double taxation.

---

[50] Brazil, (note 209), Art. 8.
[51] Brazil, (note 210), Arts. 24 and 24-A.
[52] Brazil, Ordinary Law n. 12.249/10, available at www.planalto.gov.br, last accessed on 22 June 2017, Art. 25.
[53] Brazil, (note 216), Art. 26.
[54] Brazil, Ordinary Law n. 9.249/95, Art. 25, available at www.planalto.gov.br, last accessed on 21 June 2017.

I.2.2.1. Active Income

For the definition of active income, see section I.1.1.

I.2.2.1.1. Business Profits

Profits earned abroad are subject to the general rules of the corporate income tax. This rule applies even if the income is earned through a subsidiary company and it is not distributed, as it will be seen in the section regarding the Brazilian CFC legislation. Furthermore, the resident company must also pay the social contribution on net profits, mentioned afore[55]. Income earned from the provision of services abroad is also taxed in Brazil under the general rules of the corporate income tax.

I.2.2.1.1.1. Taxable Event

The earning of income abroad

I.2.2.1.1.2. Taxable Basis

The profits earned by the business activity

I.2.2.1.1.3. Taxpayers

Brazilian resident entities

I.2.2.1.1.4. Tax rates

The same applicable on domestic situations, including the rates of 15%, the surtax of 10% and the 9% social contribution.

---

[55] See section 2.4.

I.2.2.2. Passive Income

I.2.2.2.1. Dividends

Different from the domestic situation, dividends received by a Brazilian resident from abroad are subject to taxation, as the law prescribing the dividend exemption set as a requirement that the distributing company must be subject to the actual profit or presumed profit regime[56]. Since only domiciled enterprises are taxed in accordance with these regimes, dividends distributed by non-resident enterprises to a Brazilian enterprise should be taxed.

I.2.2.2.1.1. Taxable Event
The receipt of dividends from abroad

I.2.2.2.1.2. Taxable Basis
The amount received

I.2.2.2.1.3. Taxpayers
The Brazilian resident entity

I.2.2.2.1.4. Tax rates
Since the dividends will be added to the income of the resident entity, they will be subject to the domestic rates for income taxation, 15% plus eventual surtax of 10% and the social contribution of 9%.

I.2.2.2.2. Interest
Interest sourced abroad and paid to a Brazilian entity is also taxed under the general rules of the corporate income tax.

---

[56] Brazil, (note¡**Error! Marcador no definido.**), Art. 10.

I.2.2.2.2.1. Taxable Event
The receipt of interest by the resident entity.

I.2.2.2.2.2 Taxable Basis
The interest received.

I.2.2.2.2.3. Taxpayers
The Brazilian entity recipient of the interest.

I.2.2.2.2.4. Tax rates
General rule of corporate taxation, 15% rate and, eventually, the 10% surtax and the social contribution on net profit.

I.2.2.2.3. Royalties
Similar to interest income, royalties sourced abroad are also subject to taxation in Brazil if paid to a Brazilian entity.

I.2.2.2.3.1. Taxable Event
The receipt of royalties by the resident entity.

I.2.2.2.3.2. Taxable Basis
The royalty income received.

I.2.2.2.3.3. Taxpayers
The Brazilian recipient of income.

I.2.2.2.3.4. Tax rates
General rates of income taxation, as dividends and interest.

I.2.2.3. Special Features of the CIT system

I.2.2.3.1. Existence of Group Regime

There is no group regime in Brazil with companies abroad

I.2.2.3.2. Treatment of Losses

Losses cannot be brought to Brazil but can be carried forward for future use.

I.2.2.3.3. Tax Holidays

There are no special rules regarding tax holidays for income earned by resident entities abroad.

I.2.2.3.4. Relations with Tax Havens or Low Tax Regimes

Income sourced in tax havens is not subject to a higher tax rate per se, but it may be subject to more stringent rules, specially if income is derived from dealings with related parties.

I.2.2.3.5. Relief Methods

As a rule, and in line with the system of worldwide taxation, Brazil provides a credit for taxes paid abroad.

I.3. Anti-avoidance legislation

To counteract abusive transactions, the Brazilian tax system contains a general anti-avoidance rule and specific anti-avoidance rules such as, thin cap rules and CFC rules.

These rules are normally applied in dealings between related parties, which in Brazil engulfs not only relations between parent and subsidiary companies, but also with branches, affiliated companies and between shareholders and members of the board of directors[57]. However, as mentioned afore, they are also applied in dealings with entities located in low tax jurisdictions or benefiting from a privileged fiscal regime.

I.3.1. General Anti-avoidance rule

The Brazilian general anti-avoidance rule prescribes that the tax authorities can disregard transactions entered with the goal of concealing the occurrence of a taxable event or tampering with the tax liability, with due regard to the procedures established by an ordinary law[58]. Even though this provision is part of the National Tax Code since 2001, such ordinary law has never been enacted. In the absence of the parameters to determine which situations can be disregarded, this provision should not serve as a general anti-avoidance rule. Nonetheless, in practice the tax authorities have been constantly disregarding legal transactions which they consider lacking business purpose.

I.3.2. Thin Cap rules

The Brazilian thin cap rules have been enacted in 2010 and prescribe that interest paid by a Brazilian entity to a related party not resident in a low tax regime or subject to a privileged tax regime will not be deductible if: (i) in case of debt contracted with a related party that holds an equity participation in the Brazilian company, the debt/equity ratio is higher than 2:1; (ii) in case of debt contracted with a related party that has no equity participation in the Brazilian entity, the debt/net worth ratio is higher than 2:1. In any

---

[57] Brazil, (note 210), Art. 23.
[58] Brazil, (note 171), Art. 116, sole paragraph.

case the total debt with related parties cannot surpass the 2:1 ratio as regards the total equity stake of related parties on the Brazilian entity[59].

In case the foreign entity is resident in a low-tax jurisdiction or benefits from a privileged fiscal regime, irrespective of whether it is related to the Brazilian entity, interest will only be deductible up to the 0.3:1 debt/equity ratio. [60]

I.3.3. CFC legislation

Brazil has a unique CFC legislation, since the profits of all controlled companies, irrespective of the place in which the controlled company is resident and the characterization of the income as active or passive, will be taxed in Brazil in the year they were earned, regardless of actual distribution. Hence, the rules are not actually focused on abusive conducts by the taxpayers, but rather on the fact that a Brazilian resident earned income abroad.

This system is also applied to affiliated companies as long as one of the following conditions apply: (i) the foreign company is located in a low tax jurisdiction or benefits from a privileged tax regime; or (ii) the foreign entity is subject to a tax rate lower than 20% or is controlled, directly or indirectly, by a company subject to such rate [61]. In case the affiliated company does not fulfill these conditions, the Brazilian entity will only be taxed when the income is effectively distributed[62].

Apart from the rules mentioned afore, this CFC regime also introduced two novelties in the Brazilian tax system. Provided that the foreign entity is not subject to a taxation lower than 20%, is not located in a low tax jurisdiction or

---

59 Brazil, (note 216), Art. 24.
60 Brazil, (note 216), Art. 25.
61 Brazil, Ordinary Law n. 12.973, available at www.planalto.gov.br, last accessed on 22 June 2017,
Article 82.
62 Brazil, (note 225), Article 81.

benefits from a preferential tax regime, and at least 80% of its income is considered "active income", i.e. income from the development of economic activities, excluded, inter alia, royalties, interest, dividends, the tax due may be paid in 8 yearly installments, in which the first installment would have to correspond to at least 12.5% of the tax due[63].

Furthermore, if these requirements are fulfilled and the foreign entity is located in a country which has a double tax convention/agreement with Brazil regarding the exchange of information, the accounts of the foreign subsidiaries can be, until 2022, consolidated in the Brazilian parent company[64].

I.4. Tax Treaty Law

Brazil has been signing conventions for the avoidance of double taxation since the 1960s. Nonetheless, the country does not have a broad tax treaty network, and in quite a peculiar manner it does not have tax treaties with some of its main trading partners, e.g. United States and Germany.

Additionally, even though the tax treaties include in their scope solely the income tax, Brazil has recently made clear that the social contribution on net profit is also under the scope of the treaties[65].

I.4.1. Adherence to UN or OECD Model Convention

The Brazilian tax treaties are modelled based on the structure present in the OECD model tax convention, but they contain more source taxing rights than the former. Hence, it can be said that the treaties are more in line with the UN Model Convention.

---

[63] Brazil, (note 225), Articles. 90-91.

[64] Brazil, (note 225), Article 78.

[65] Brazil, Ordinary Law n. 13.202/15, available at www.planalto.gov.br, last accessed on 23 June 2017.

I.4.2. Special Features Commonly present on Tax Treaties

In Brazilian tax treaties royalties are taxed at source and the "other income" article also allows for taxation at source. On that matter, in most Brazilian DTCs the definition of royalties includes the provision of technical services. Additionally, despite the deletion of Article 14 by the OECD model convention, Brazil continues to include this provision on its tax treaties.

Moreover, a considerable number of the the Brazilian DTCs contain provisions on tax sparing/matching credit, guaranteeing that eventual tax benefits given to taxpayers are not annulled by a consequent increase of taxation in the residence state of the income earner. Further, clauses regarding limitations on benefits are not widespread, but they are constantly being adopted in the most recent treaties.

I.4.3. Treaties currently in force

At the moment there are 33 tax treaties in force, which are, in the chronological order in which they were signed: (i) Brazil-Japan (1967); (ii) Brazil-France (1971); (iii) Brazil-Belgium (1972); (iv) Brazil-Denmark (1974); (v) Brazil-Spain (1974); (vi) Brazil-Sweden (1975); (vii) Brazil-Austria (1975); (viii) Brazil-Italy (1978); (ix) Brazil-Luxembourg (1978); (x) Brazil-Argentina (1980); (xi) Brazil-Norway (1980); (xii) Brazil-Ecuador (1983); (xiii) Brazil-Philippines (1983); (xiv) Brazil-Canada (1984); (xv) Brazil-Hungary (1986); (xvi) Brazil-Czech Republic (1986); (xvii) Brazil-Slovakia (1986); (xviii) Brazil-India (1988); (xix) Brazil-South Korea (1989); (xx) Brazil-The Netherlands (1990); (xxi) Brazil-China (1991); (xxii) Brazil-Finland (1996); (xxiii) Brazil-Portugal (2000); (xxiv) Brazil-Chile (2001); (xxv) Brazil-Ukraine (2002); (xxvi) Brazil-Israel (2002); (xxvii) Brazil-Mexico (2003); (xxviii) Brazil-South Africa (2003);

(xxix) Brazil-Venezuela (2005); (xxx) Brazil-Peru (2006); (xxxi) Brazil-Trinidad & Tobago (2008); and (xxxii) Brazil-Turkey.

I.5. Community Law

Despite the size of its economy, Brazil is still an outlier regarding participation in economic unions.

I.5.1. Participation in a Community/Union

Brazil is a founding member of the MERCOSUR and is a member of the Community of Portuguese Speaking Countries. These groups do not have specific legislation or jurisprudence affecting the corporate income tax levied in Brazil.

I.6. Influence of BEPS Action Plan in the country

Brazil is part of the BEPS Inclusive framework, so amendments are being discussed in its legislation based on the BEPS Action Plan.

I.6.1. Adoption of rules in line with BEPS Reports

Since the release of the BEPS reports, Brazil has tackled some of the issues raised on BEPS actions 5[66], 13[67] and 14[68]. It also tried to implement rules in line with BEPS action 12, but this was not approved by the Congress.

---

[66] Instrução Normativa n. 1681/2016, available at www.receita.fazenda.gov.br, last accessed on 23 June 2017.
[67] Instrução Normativa n. 1681/2016, available at www.receita.fazenda.gov.br, last accessed on 23 June 2017.
[68] Instrução Normativa n. 1689/2017, available at www.receita.fazenda.gov.br, last accessed on 23 June 2017.

I.6.2. Participation in multilateral instrument

Brazil was a member of the ad hoc group that drafted the multilateral instrument, but it opted not to sign the MLI. Instead, Brazil is aiming to amend its tax treaties through individual negotiation with the countries.

I.7. Jurisprudence

Brazil does not have vast jurisprudence regarding international aspects of its legislation, but there has been considerable discussion on the validity of its CFC rules, which, as mentioned afore, are broad.

The rule was questioned in 2002, but it was only in 2013 that the Supreme Court ruled that the Brazilian CFC regime could be applied in case of controlled companies located in tax havens or fiscal privileged regimes, but not in case of affiliated companies located elsewhere[69]. In a subsequent case the court clarified that the regime could also be applied for controlled companies not located in tax havens or fiscal privileged regimes[70].

Furthermore, the Superior Court of Justice (highest court in non-constitutional matters) has subsequently ruled that if Brazil has signed a tax treaty with the state in which the controlled foreign company is located, profits of this companies can only be taxed therein, irrespective of the Brazilian CFC rules.

---

[69] ADI 2.588/DF, available at www.stf.jus.br, last accessed on 30 July 2017.
[70] RE 541.090/SC, available at www.stf.jus.br, last accessed on 30 July 2017.

4

Colombia[1]

DR. ESPERANZA BUITRAGO DIAZ • MR. JUAN RAFAEL BRAVO

I.1 Corporate Income Tax at Domestic level

Corporate taxes in Colombia are imposed at the national and local levels. Nowadays the term corporate taxation in Colombia includes the income tax, wealth tax, and the trade tax. A solidarity income tax (CREE) was also in force from 2013 until 2016. Given the scope of this work, our report only covers the Corporate Income Tax (CIT). At the end of the work readers find a table with the main features of other taxes. In Colombia, the CIT includes all kind of taxes whose calculation is based on income, capital gains as well as business profits for branches of foreign corporations and entities (article 5 Tax Statute, hereinafter TS[2]).

---

[1]   Special acknowledgements are due to the Maastricht Centre for Taxation and to the Max Planck Institute for Tax Law and Public Finance for the time and resources made available for this report to Dr. Esperanza Buitrago. Also to PWC Colombia for the complementary access to the Tax Statute online.

[2]   The laws on national taxes and tax procedures are compiled in the so-called TS (Decree 624/1989, its addendums and reforms). This Statute compiles the regulations of the taxes administered by DIAN: income tax, CREE, wealth tax, withholding taxes, VAT, GMF.

I.1.1. Active Income

I.1.1.1. Business Profits

CIT is imposed on domestic and foreign corporations. However, whilst Colombian corporations are taxed on their worldwide income, foreign corporations and legal entities (branches and PEs) are taxed only on income and occasional gains of Colombian sources as defined by the TS, mainly (but not limited to): 1) Profits derived by Colombian companies; 2) the transfer or exploitation of tangible and intangible property located in Colombia; 3) the transfer of goods produced in the country, regardless of the place of transfer; the rendering of services in Colombia; 4) the rendering of technical assistance and consulting services, as well as the execution of turnkey contracts, within or outside Colombia (for an extensive list, see 1.2 below).

For residents, the concept and scope of the source rules determine the deductibility of foreign expenses and tax credits.

I.1.1.1.1. Taxable Event

The CIT taxable event is the reception of ordinary and extraordinary income derived in the taxable year that is likely to produce a net increase in equity (patrimony), at the time of their perception. For occasional gains, the taxable event is the windfall of revenues.

I.1.1.1.2. Taxable Basis

The taxable income is determined considering the sum of all ordinary and extraordinary income made in the taxable year that: 1) are likely to produce a net increase in equity at the time of realization, 2) have not been expressly excluded. To calculate the taxable income it is necessary to subtract from the gross income the returns, rebates, ordinary costs incurred in the generation of net income as well as all deductions allowed. Expenses deemed necessary for obtaining taxable income may be deducted if the general conditions for deductibility are met. Taxpayers may deduct the expenses in which they incurred abroad provided that: 1) the expense is necessary (has a causal relationship to income from Colombian sources), 2) the withholding tax was made whenever the payment is taxable income in Colombia for its beneficiary and, 3) there is proof of the withholding (Articles 121, 122 TS). Registration of the contract before the Ministry of Commerce, Industry and Tourism is not required for withholding tax purposes. The Tax Administration (DIAN) considers it mandatory, however.

TS Article	Deductions	Income Tax
107	Necessary expenses	X
108	Wages only when para fiscal contributions have been paid.	X
108-1	Payments to widows and orphans from armed forces members killed in combat, kidnapped or missing	X
108-3	Card handling fees	X
109	Severance paid	X
110	Consolidated severance	X
111	Retirement and disability pensions	X
112	Provision for the payment of future pensions.	X
114	Contributions to the Colombian Family Welfare Institute, National Learning Service (SENA) and family subsidy	X
115	Paid Taxes. 100% of the Industry and Commerce Tax and property tax. 50% of the financial transactions tax	X

116	Taxes, royalties and contributions paid by decentralized bodies	X
117	Interest	X
118	The inflationary component of interests is not deductible	X
119	Interest on loans for house purchase	X
120	Adjustments for exchange differences	X
121	Expenses abroad	X
122	Limitation of cost and deductions	X
124	Payment to the head office	X
124-1	Other non-deductible payments	X
124-2	Payments to tax heavens	X
125	Donations	X
126	Contributions to mutual funds	X
126-1	Contributions to disability and retirement pension funds and unemployment funds.	X
126-2	Donations to foundations and corporations dedicated to the defense, protection and promotion of human rights and access to justice	X
126-5	Donations for natural parks and natural forests	X
127-1	Leasing contracts	X
128	Depreciations	X
129	Obsolescence in depreciable assets	X
142	Amortization of investments	X
145	Provision for doubtful or difficult collection debts	X
146	Manifestly lost or worthless debts	X
147	Compensation of tax losses of companies	X

148	Loss of assets due to force majeure	X
149	losses on alienation of assets	X
151	Non-deductibility for losses in sales of assets to related parties	X
152	Non-deductibility for losses in sales of assets from a company to their shareholders	X
153	Non-deductibility for losses in sales of shares and contributions	X
154 y 155	Non-deductibility of bonds	X
157	New investments in plantations, irrigation, wells and silos	X
158	Amortization in the agricultural sector	X
158-1	Investments in scientific and technological development	X
158-2	Investments in control and improvement of the environment	X
159	Investments in the oil industry and mining sector.	X
160	Hydrocarbons exploration in contracts in existence at 28 of October 1974	X
161	Exhaustion of exploitation of hydrocarbons in contracts in existence at 28 of October 1974	X
166	Special deduction on exploitation of hydrocarbons	X
167	Exhaustion in exploitation of mines, gases different from hydrocarbons and natural gas deposits	X
171	amortization of investments in gas and mineral explorations	X
173	In reforestation plantations	X
174	Sums paid as annuity	X

176	For the livestock business	X
177	Limitation of costs are applicable to deductions	X
177-2	Common costs and expenses limitations.	X

Expenses incurred abroad are deductible if they are associated with getting domestic source income (article 121 TS) and there are limited to 15% of the taxpayer's net income, calculated before the discount of such costs or deductions (article 122 TS). Some expenses are deductible without restraining to the 15% limit mentioned, *e.g.* 1) payments subject to withholding tax, 2) short-term loans for the imports of goods and bank overdrafts, 3) appropriations made for financing or pre-financing exports, 4) payments made to brokers located outside Colombia for the purchase of goods or raw material up to certain amount determined by the government, 5) interest paid on short-term loans acquired to finance the import or export of goods if certain requirements are met, 6) payments that are not of Colombian source; 7) expenses related to the reparation and maintenance of equipment abroad, 8) the training of personnel services provided abroad to public entities, 9) payments for the purchase of tangible goods; 10) costs and expenses capitalized for future depreciation, and 11) costs and expenses related to the compliance of legal obligations. Direct or indirect payments made to foreign parent companies or offices for management, royalties and exploitation or purchase of intangibles are deductible as a general rule, provided the corresponding withholding was applied, if mandatory and if such transaction comply with transfer pricing rules.

Nondeductible expenses include dividends, expenses that are deemed not to have a causal relationship with the production of income, income tax and VAT, net worth tax, registration tax, stamp tax and vehicle tax. Payments to related individuals or legal entities located, incorporated or operating in tax havens are deductible as long as the taxpayer (if it is a related party) complies with the documentation indicated in article 260-7-3 TS concerning the transfer pricing regime.

The foreign WHT is creditable against the final income tax liability of Colombian residents if the foreign tax does not exceed the tax which would have been due in Colombia on that income. Income from Colombian sources derived by foreign companies without a permanent presence in Colombia is subject to WHT. If the withholding is applied a tax declaration is not required.

In the determination of the taxable income in Colombia is important to stress that corporations and entities are also expected to establish their taxable income according to an alternative "presumptive income" system. In this case, the minimum taxable income must be equal

to at least 3,5% of the company's tax equity determined as of 31 December of the immediately preceding calendar year. The income tax applies to the higher of the net income or the presumptive income.

I.1.1.1.3. Taxpayers

Corporate income tax is imposed on:

1. Domestic corporations and entities having their effective place of management in Colombian territory in the taxable year or period (irrespective of incorporation abroad, DIAN *Concepto* 61818 of 2014). As to the law that is the place where the decisive and necessary commercial and management decisions to carry out the activities of the corporation or entity as a whole are taken.

   Foreign corporations that have issued stock or bonds in the Colombian stock exchange or in a recognized foreign stock exchange are not considered to have their effective place of management in Colombia. The subsidiaries of such companies are also not considered to have their effective place of management in Colombia to the extent that there is consolidation in the financial statements of the parent. Such subsidiaries can elect to be treated as a national corporation unless they are 80% Foreign Income Companies.

2. Corporations or entities having their main domicile in Colombian territory,

3. Corporations or entities incorporated in Colombia according to Colombian law,

4. Permanent establishments (hereinafter PEs) as defined for domestic tax purposes, i.e. a fixed place of business located in Colombia through which a foreign company or a non-resident individual performs all or part of its activities. Colombian tax law provides the following list of examples: branches, agencies, offices, workshops, mines, oil or gas wells, or any other place involving the extraction or exploitation of natural resources. Independent agents and activities of ancillary or preparatory character (as defined by Decree 3026, 2013) are excluded from the scope of the definition. In a number of rulings the Colombian Revenue Service (DIAN) stated cases that do not configure a PE, for instance a foreign portfolio investment (DIAN, Oficio 5468 of 2016). Representative offices of foreign financial institutions whose only purpose is to promote or advertise services do not constitute PEs due to the ancillary and preparatory character of the activities (DIAN, OFICIO N° 029266 of 2014). Permanent Establishments are required to get a tax number, present tax returns and the income taxable in Colombia follows the rules of the force of attraction if the income is deemed to be of Colombian source (Decree 3026, 2013).

5. Non-resident companies and entities are subject to CIT depending on whether they perform their activities directly, through a branch or a permanent establishment. If the latter is the case, branches are subject to the same rules as

residents but are taxed only on their income from domestic source. Branches of foreign companies that derive income in Colombia must file tax declarations.

6. Foreign companies deriving more than 80% of their income (other than passive income) in the jurisdiction of incorporation are not considered to have their effective place of management in Colombia. Article 12, paragraph 5 TS rules the 80% calculation of income generated abroad.

7. A special regime (hereinafter CITS) applies to nonprofit organizations meeting certain requirements and as long as they are not excluded by the law.

Enterprise collaboration agreements such as consortiums, joint ventures, unincorporated temporary joint ventures are not subject to the CIT themselves. Instead, each of the parties bear the tax liability.

I.1.1.1.4. Tax rates

The corporate income tax rates vary depending on whether corporations or entities are located in the Colombian Free Trade Zones (FTZ). In the FTZ the CIT is 20%[3](but 15% in Cucuta). Out of the FTZ a 34 or 33% apply, as follows:

Corporate Income Tax Rate	34% in 2017, 33% as from 2018
Corporate Income Tax Surtax	6% for 2017, 4% for 2018, none in 2019 (on taxable income in excess of 800 million Colombian pesos, hereinafter COP).
Capital Gains Tax Rate	10%
Branch and PE Tax Rate	34%

---

[3] Other incentives in force in the Free Trade Zones include exemptions of VAT and custom duties.

I.1.2. Passive Income

I.1.2.1. Dividends

The taxation of dividends varies depending on whether the dividends are paid between domestic companies, Andean Community companies, or in inbound or outbound situations. Dividends received by a domestic company from another domestic company are not subject to CIT if the distributing company has already paid taxes on the profits distributed. The portion of dividends distributed by an Andean MNE corresponding to profits earned by a branch in another Andean Member State will not be taxed in the country of the headquarters.

From FY 2017 onwards, dividend distribution is taxed; this means that only dividends paid out of profits obtained in FY 2017 should be subject to the dividend tax

I.1.2.1.1. Taxable Event

The concept and taxable event is defined in article 30 of the TS, as any distribution of benefits, in money or in kind, in charge to the company's equity that is made to partners, shareholders, members, associates, subscribers or similar, except for capital reductions and share placement premiums. It is also defined as any transfer of profits corresponding to occasional gains from national source, from permanent establishments or branches in Colombia from non-resident persons, to related parties abroad.

I.1.2.1.2. Taxable Basis

Amount of dividends distributed to the tax payer.

I.1.2.1.3. Taxpayers

According to articles 48 and 49 TS, dividends are taxed in the hands of the shareholders of Colombian companies.

I.1.2.1.4. Tax rates

This tax is applied regardless of the profits being taxed or not at the distributing company level, and the rates differ depending on the residence of the beneficiary.

For a resident company, dividends are not taxed if profits out of which the dividends are paid, already have been taxed at the corporate level. Dividends out of profits not taxed at the corporate level, are taxed at a rate of 33%.

I.1.2.2. Interest

Income from interests is subject to the general rules of the CIT described before.

I.1.2.2.1. Taxable Event

See section I.1.1.1.1.

I.1.2.2.2. Taxable Basis

See section I.1.1.1.2.

I.1.2.2.3. Taxpayers

See section I.1.1.1.3.

I.1.2.2.4. Tax rates

See section I.1.1.1.4.

I.1.2.3. Royalties

Income from royalties is subject to the general rules of the CIT describe before.

I.1.2.3.1. Taxable Event

See section I.1.1.1.1.

I.1.2.3.2. Taxable Basis

See section I.1.1.1.2.

I.1.2.3.3. Taxpayers

See section I.1.1.1.3.

I.1.2.3.4. Tax rates

See section I.1.1.1.4.

I.1.3. Special Features of the CIT system

I.1.3.1. Existence of Group Regime

Colombian tax law does not have a group regime.

I.1.3.2. Treatment of Losses

Losses may be offset against the income generated in the following 12 years, unless they relate to: 1) Losses related to proceeds that are not considered income or occasional gains, 2) costs or deductions not related to the generation of taxable income. Tax losses generated until 2016 could be carried forward without time limitation. Carryback is not possible.

Losses not deductible include: 1) losses related to the alienation of assets to related parties; 2) losses related to the alienation of assets whenever the transaction takes place between the limited company or assimilated company and its partners (provided they are individuals or not settled successions, the spouse, relatives of the partners within the fourth degree of consanguinity and the second of affinity or only civil one; 3) losses related to the alienation of shares or quotas of social interest and 4) loses related to the alienation of special financial bonds;

I.1.3.3. Tax Holidays

Tax holidays related to the CIT include mainly the regime applicable in the Free Trade Zones (FTZ), reduction of statutory CIT rates, exemptions, tax free mergers and demergers, and a special tax credit on payroll payments.

I.1.3.3.1. Free Trade Zones

Industrial enterprises located at the FTZ enjoy a 20% CIT on income derived from the FTZ operations. By exception Cucuta has a 15% CIT rate. Capital Gains are taxed at a rate of 10%. For commercial users apply a 34% CIT and as from 2017 the CIT is 33%.

I.1.3.3.2. Reduced statutory CIT rate for SMEs

SMEs within certain brackets are subject to a reduced CIT rate of about 9% for five years applicable either from the moment they started their operation, or from the moment in which they obtain taxable income.

I.1.3.3.3. Exemptions of the CIT

As from 2018 income exempted from CIT includes: 1) income exempt under AC Directive 578, 2) funds of the pension system, 3) amounts due, interests, commissions and other financial interest due by official entities of financial character as well as of cooperation entities ,for the development from countries to which Colombia has signed cooperation agreements, 4) income from the use of foreign plantations, investments in new sawmill related to the new plantation, 5) income from donations or aid to entities to foreign governments, 6) Income from the sale of electric power generated from wind, biomass, or agricultural waste, for a period of 15 years, as long as a) the seller issues and negotiates Greenhouse Gas Reduction Certificates in accordance with Kyoto's Protocol and b) 50% of the income obtained in the sale of the certificates is invested in social projects of the region in which the generator operates, 7) income related to social housing or priority interest according to the conditions set by law, 8) Income obtained from hotel services offered in new hotels built within 15 years counted from 2017. This exemption is available for a term of 30 years.

The following tax exemptions of the CIT are only available up to 2017: 1) income from river transport services with shallow drafts, 2) Income obtained from hotel services offered in refurbished or enlarged hotel facilities, provided that certain conditions are met. 3) Leasing agreements with option to purchase real state built for sale, 4) Income obtained from ecotourism services, 5) a kind of patent box consisting or an exemption of income derived from new medicinal and software products developed in Colombia and patented in Colombia.

I.1.3.3.4. No taxation of mergers and demergers

Mergers and demergers are free of tax provided that the following conditions are met: 1) the surviving entity or the beneficiary entity is a resident, 2) de-mergers are over units of business/going concern (substance requirement), 3) the value of the shares received by shareholders owning at least 75% (85% for related parties) is proportional to the one prior to the merger or de-merger., 4) the shareholders receive at least 90% of value in shares (99% if participants are related), 5) The income tax due for the sale is increased on a 30% whenever the shareholders sell the shares received within two years of the merger/de-merger. The above mentioned also apply if the participants are not residents if the assets held in Colombia represent 20% or less of the worldwide aggregate of assets of the group.

I.1.3.3.5. Tax credit on payroll payments

Employers hiring any of the following persons benefit from a tax credit: 1) individuals below 28 years old, 2) women above 40 years old provided that they have not been legally employed in the previous year; 3) workers earning less than 1.5 times the minimum monthly wage (around COP 1,106,576); 4) disabled persons, persons reintegrated to democracy (from the military conflict), or displaced persons as consequence of the internal conflict in the conditions stated by the law.

I.1.3.3.6. Special new investments

- New investments in environmental preservation control and enhancements are subject to a 25% deduction provided that certain conditions are met. (article 255 TS)

- Full deductions for qualified research and technology development projects if certain conditions are met.

Other deductions are indicated in I.1.1.1.2.

I.2. Corporate Income Tax on International Level

Considering that resident corporations and entities are subject to income tax on their worldwide income whilst non-resident companies, including their local branches, are only taxed on their Colombian-source income, the concepts of residence and source play an important role at the international level.

Non-residents are taxed depending on whether they perform their activities directly, through a branch or a permanent establishment. If the latter is the case, branches are subject to the same rules as residents but are taxed only on their income from domestic source. Branches of foreign companies that derive income in Colombia must file tax declarations. Permanent Establishments are required to get a tax number, to keep accounting books, and to submit tax returns. PE's taxable income in Colombia follows the force of attraction rule if the income is deemed to be of Colombian source (Decree 1625, 2016). For purposes of attribution of profits to the PE it is necessary to have a study of functions, assets, risks and personal involved in the generation of income or perception of gains. Whenever the head office performs activities in Colombia that are not attributable to its branch or PE, the proceeds not attributable are subject to a withholding tax of 33%.

The TS defines PE´s for domestic purposes as a fixed place of business located in Colombia through which a foreign company or a non-resident individual performs all or part of its activities. The following are included in the exemplificative list: branches, agencies, offices, workshops, mines, oil or gas wells, or any other place involving the extraction or exploitation of natural resources. Independent agents and activities of ancillary or preparatory character as well as representation offices of foreign reinsurance companies are excluded from the scope of the definition. Tax treaties may contain different definitions.

The decisive criteria to determine whether companies and entities are residents for CIT purposes is the place of effective management in Colombian territory during the taxable year or period. Such criteria include 1) the place wherein business and management decisions, which are decisive and necessary to carry out the activities of the company or legal entity as a whole, are made; 2) having their domicile in Colombian territory; and 3) incorporation under Colombian law[4]. In order to establish if there is residence, a factual test applies. Special attention is paid to facts related to the places where senior executives and managers of the company usually exercise their responsibilities and carry out the daily activities of the company's upper management. If a company has its effective place of management in Colombia it needs to keep a tax number of registration (so called RUT) and accounting records in accordance with the Colombian regime.

Notwithstanding the above, the law establishes that foreign companies won't be considered residents even if its place of effective management is in Colombia, whenever they: 1) issue bonds or stock in the Colombian stock exchange (*Bolsa de Valores*) or in a qualified foreign stock exchange according to an administrative ordinance issued by the DIAN. Likewise, in the case of subsidiaries of a parent company that issues bonds

---

4   Although foreign companies conducting regular business in Colombia are statutorily required to set up a local branch, they are subject to income tax only on their Colombian-source income.

or stock as explained above, as long as the subsidiary has its financial statements consolidated with its parent company. A list of stock exchanges that are recognized for applying the exception to the rule of effective place of management for foreign entities is set by Administrative Regulation 57 of 2016 provides; and 2) foreign companies that obtain 80% or more of their income in their country of incorporation. Passive income (like interest and royalties) shall not be considered for determining this percentage. Dividends obtained directly or indirectly will be considered passive income as long as they are derived from direct or indirect participations of 25% or less in the capital of the foreign company.

The concept of source is fundamental and the law indicates the cases in which the income derived is deemed to be of Colombian source. Article 24 TS states, amongst other cases: 1. Transfer or exploitation of tangible and intangible goods located within Colombian territory; 2. Transfer of goods within Colombian territory; 3. Rendering of services within Colombian territory; 4. Rendering of technical services, technical assistance and consulting services, and the undersigning of turn-key contracts, inside and outside Colombia; 5. Earning of profits by Colombian companies; 6. Returns on credits owned in Colombia; 6. The profits from manufacturing or industrial processing of goods or raw materials within the country, irrespective of the place of sale or disposal; 7. Income derived from commercial activities within Colombia; 8. For the contractor of "turnkey" contracts and other contracts for the preparation of material works, the total value of the respective contract; 9. In general terms, foreign source income includes any revenues arising from the transfer or exploitation of tangible and intangible goods located outside of Colombia, and the rendering of services abroad. Furthermore, income generated upon certain foreign loans is not deemed as local source income.

I.2.1. Inbound Transactions

Inbound payments received by Colombian corporations are part of the CIT taxable base in the same manner as income of Colombian sources. Inbound dividends are part of the taxable base from the income tax and CREE and the taxpayer has the right to a tax discount that works as an ordinary tax credit applicable to the CIT (Article 254 TS) and CREE (Article 22-5, Law 1606, 2012).

1.2.1.1 Business profits

Foreign-source income and capital gains obtained by individuals, corporations or assimilated entities through a branch or PE are subject to CIT and surtax (depending on the taxable year CREE may also apply). The attribution of profits takes into account the risks, functions, assets and personnel involved whilst obtaining the income.

1.2.1.2 Inbound dividends

Inbound dividend are included in the general taxable base and treated as ordinary income. A tax credit is available in the terms previously mentioned.

1.2.1.3. Interest, royalties and other income

These types of passive income are included in the general taxable base and follow the same rules of other revenues. A tax credit is available in the terms above mentioned.

I.2.1.4. Capital gains

The capital gains tax is levied on the actual disposal of fixed assets owned for more than 2 years (for lower periods of time such gains are treated as ordinary income), on inheritances, donations, the benefits of the surviving spouse, the liquidation of legal entities that have existed for more than

2 years, and prizes from lotteries, raffles and profits. Special rules apply for the calculation of the capital gains for each of the cases indicated. Capital gains can only be compensated with capital losses. Domestic tax law does not set provisions for a deferral of the capital gains tax.

I.2.2. Outbound Transactions

1.2.1.1 Withholdings applicable

Outbound transactions are subject to withholding taxes if income is from domestic source. The main withholdings applicable to cross border transactions are as follows:

General clause Income derived from		Fee for payments	
Exploitation of material and intangible goods	Within Colombia	Royalties or exploitation of industrial property or know-how. Profits or royalties derived from literary, artistic or scientific work	15% of the nominal value of the payment/CA
		Exploitation of cinematographic films	15% of the gross value of the payment/CA
		Exploitation of computer software	33% on 80% of the payment/CA

Alienation of material or intangible goods	Located within the country by the time of its alienation	Occasional gains (art. 415 ITA) Rate for profits or exploitation of industrial or intellectual property (art. 408 ITA)	10% on the gross value of the payment/CA 15% of the nominal value of the payment/CA
Licensing services or right to use software	Inbound payments to Colombian taxpayers subject to IT in Colombia	Licensing services or right to use software	3.5% of the payment/CA
Provision of services	Within Colombia Permanent or temporary With or without and establishment	Provision of services and technical assistance Technical services provided by non-resident persons	15% of the nominal value of the payment
Turnkey contracts	When the contractors are foreign companies or entities without domicile in Colombia, natural persons without residence in Colombia or illiquid successions from persons not residing in the country at the time of his death		1% of the value of the contract
Interest			15% of the payment

Payments to tax heavens	When the beneficiary is an individual or any kind of entities created, located or functioning in tax heavens		33% of the payment (34% in 2017)
Dividends		Dividends paid to foreign companies or entities without domicile in Colombia. Dividend is attributable to a permanent establishment or branch resident in Colombia from the foreign entity (article 246TS)	5% if such dividends and participations were taxed at the level of the Company. 38.25% if such dividends were not taxed
Others		Cases without a specific provision	15% on the gross value of the payment

I.2.2.2 Business profits

Foreign entities are taxed on the business profits related to operations directly attributable to their Colombian branch or PE on their income from Colombian sources. When the head office performs activities in the country directly, which are different from those attributable to its branch or PE, the head office is subject to withholding tax at a rate of 33%.

Some payments to parent companies are not deductible, for instance 1) interest and other financial expenses unless they comply with the transfer princing rules or are owed to financial entities under the supervision of the Financial Superintendence, 2) payments to residents of low tax or preferential jurisdictions, unless the 33%

withholding was applied and there was a transfer pricing analysis. This does not apply to financial transactions registered at the Central Bank, 3) capital losses derived from the transfer of assets between related parties or from the alienation of shares or partnership interests.

The transfer pricing rules apply to transactions between the PE and the head office or related parties.

I.2.2.3 Dividends, interest and royalties

Dividends, interest and royalties earned by non-residents through a Colombian branch are included in the taxable base of the branch and subject to tax at the general rate. The withholding tax and rates on outbound payments are indicated in 1.2.1.1.

I.2.2.4 Special features

I.2.2.4.1. Relief Methods

Under domestic tax law an ordinary tax credit is available for taxes paid abroad provided that the income is of foreign source and the tax does not exceed the amounts applicable in Colombia on the same income. The calculation of the tax credit follows the formula set by article 254 TS. The value of the discount equals the result of multiplying the amount of dividends or participations by the income tax rate on which the utilities that generated those dividends or participations has been subjected abroad, multiplied by the following proportion:

- In the case of the CIT:

$$Applicable\ Proportion = \left(\frac{TRyC}{TRyC + TCREE + STCREE} \right)$$

- In the case of the CREE

$$Applicable\ Proportion = \left(\frac{TCREE + STCREE}{TRyC + TCREE + STCREE}\right)$$

Where

- TRyC is the tax rate of the Income tax applicable to the taxpayer for the foreign source income.
- TCREE is the tax rate of the CREE applicable to the taxpayer for the foreign source income.
- STCREE is the tax rate of the surcharge of the CREE applicable to the taxpayer for the foreign source income.

Considering that as from 2017 the CREE is no longer in force, dividends paid to a resident will be included in the taxable income of the recipient and taxed at a rate of 34% for 2017 and 33% for 2018. The tax credit will be equal to the amount paid abroad but limited to the amount of tax to be paid in Colombia.

I.2.2.4.2. Tax havens

Colombian tax law no longer refers to tax havens. Instead, the law adopted the OECD terminology of non-cooperative, low tax jurisdictions and preferential regimes. The law set a list of criteria for the government to consider whilst issuing the list of non-cooperative jurisdictions: 1) the lack of tax rates or the existence of low income nominal rates compared to the applicable ones in Colombia for similar transactions, 2) the lack of effective exchange of information or the existence of legal rules or administrative practices restraining it, 3) the lack of legal, regulatory or administrative functioning transparency, 4) the absence of substantive local presence, the exercise of a real activity

and economic substance and 5) any other criteria internationally accepted to establish whether a jurisdiction is non-
cooperative, low or zero tax jurisdiction. In 2013 and 2014
the law issued a list of tax haven jurisdictions. The list can
be updated from time to time by the Government. The law
presumes a preferential regime whenever two of the criteria
listed in numbers 1 to 4 are met, or a jurisdiction offer tax
benefits only to non-resident entities or individuals exclud-
ing its own residents of the application of the law.

Transactions with residents of the abovementioned
jurisdictions are subject to the transfer-pricing regime irrespective of whether the parties are related or not. Hence,
taxpayers are requested to file a transfer pricing study
and a transfer pricing return for transactions above 10,000
taxable units. If the transactions is between related parties, the taxpayer is required to provide a transfer pricing
study including functions performed, assets used and risks
assumed, costs and expenses related to the provision of
the service from the non-cooperative jurisdiction. Furthermore, a 33% withholding tax applies as from 2018 (34%
until 2017), for any payment or proceed that constitutes
taxable income.

I.2.2.4.3. Tax Returns for non-residents

Nonresidents are required to file a tax return whenever: 1)
the entire income of Colombian sources is not income from
dividends, interests, commissions, fees, royalties, compen-
sations for personal services, exploitation of intellectual
property (including motion pictures and software), know
how, technical assistance, technical services, consultancy, 2)
the withholding taxes have not been made for payments
of dividends, interest, commissions, fees, royalties, personal
services, exploitation of intellectual property, know-how,
technical assistance services or technical services, and 3)

the alienation of shares or quotas in Colombian companies (in addition to the cancelation of the foreign investment at the Central Bank.

I.3. Anti-Avoidance Legislation

Anti-avoidance provisions in Colombia are evolving. As from 2016 there is a general anti-avoidance clause (Article 364-1 TS), a specific antiabuse provision for nonprofit organizations (article 364-2 TS) and the law set as a crime the failure to include assets or the inclusion of non-existent liabilities (article 434A). Taxpayers that willfully omit assets or submit inaccurate information on such assets or that declare non-existent liabilities up to an amount equal or higher than 7.250 minimum monthly salaries with an impact in its CIT may be imprisoned for about 48 to 108 months and a penalty equivalent to 200% of the value of the asset omitted, of the value of the asset inaccurately declared or of the value of the non-existing liability, unless the taxpayers presents or corrects the tax return or later returns and pay if that were the case.

The new special provision anti abuse states that the CITS neither applies to nonprofit organizations abusing the legal configuration to defraud the tax law applicable, nor to sham transactions or to inexistent business. In these cases, the law allows the Revenue Service to: 1) declare the existence of the abovementioned behaviors, only for tax purposes, without the need of judicial intervention, and 2) to re-characterize and recalculate the taxes due, the default interest and the penalties for inaccuracy. The provision applies irrespective of whether the situation involves taxpayers or non-taxpayers and also presumes that a business structure constitutes abuse, fraud or simulation in the following cases:

The main purpose of the entity is an economic exploitation targeting the direct or indirect distribution of surpluses, instead of serving a general interest through the performance of meritorious activities.

Availability or possibility to access special benefits or conditions to access the goods or services offered by the entity, by the founders, partners, statutory representatives, members of the bodies of direction, spouses or relatives up to the fourth degree of consanguinity of any of them as well as any entity or person with whom any of the aforementioned persons has the status of related economic party in accordance with Articles 260-1 and 450 of the Tax Statute Possibility to access special benefits or conditions to access the goods or services offered by the entity, to

The direct or indirect acquisition of goods or services acquired directly or indirectly by founders, associates, statutory representatives, members of the governing bodies, spouses or relatives up to and including the fourth degree of any of them, as well as any other entity or person with whom any of the aforementioned persons is a related party in the terms of articles 260-1 and 450TS.

The acquisition of the right to participate in the economic results of the entity directly or through person or interposed entity as a consequence of consideration for the work of the founders, associates, statutory representatives and members of the governing body or any employment relationship contracted by the entity.

The perception of allegedly donations, money, goods or services that the nonprofit entity compensates directly or indirectly to the donor. Such amounts will be taxed as income different to the one of the entity's purpose without possibility to deduct the payments from the CITS.

Before the abovementioned legislation was in force, as well as a GAAR was introduced in 2012, the Constitutional Court in 1996 acknowledged the possibility for the DIAN to apply the "abuse of legal forms" and "legal fraud", whenever there was any indication that the taxpayer used some legal clothing to reduce its tax burden by keeping the taxable event from occurring and where the transaction itself lacks any economic substance (CC, C – 15 of 1993 and C -540). The Court held that this power of DIAN is based upon the application of the constitutional principles of substance over form (Article 228) and equitable application of taxes (Article 363). Such interpretation of the Colombian Constitutional Court is not binding since it does not have *erga omnes* effects because it was included in the considerations of the judgments and not in the decision per se. Legally such case could be considered jus an auxiliary criterion for judicial activity (Article 48 of Law 270 of 96 and Article 23 of Regulation 2067 of 1991.

Based on the abovementioned decisions, DIAN issued the Ruling 51,977 of August 2, 2005 instructing tax officials to establish that an abuse of legal forms has taken place in any case of tax evasion or avoidance, re-characterizing the transactions so that the taxable event occurs, and imposing a fine for inaccurate reporting equal to 160% of the related tax deficiency. Now, despite that these types of rulings are binding upon the tax administration, tax advisers felt they were neither binding upon the taxpayers nor upon the tax courts.

I.3.1. Abuse of Law

According to the 2016 Colombian GAAR, article 869TS, the abuse of law for tax purposes regards transactions or series of transactions involving the use or implementation of one or more artificial acts or legal transactions without economic or commercial purpose to obtain a tax advantage irrespective of any subjective intention. The law defines artificiality and tax advantage as follows:

A tax advantage is taken by the alteration, the disfigurement or modification of the tax effects that would otherwise be generated on a taxpayers or beneficial owner, as for instance the elimination, reduction or deferral of the tax, an increase in the credit balance or of the tax losses as well as the extension of tax benefits or exemptions.

Artificiality is presumed whenever 1) the transaction is not sound (reasonable) in economic or commercial terms, 2) the legal act or business results in a high tax benefit not reflected in the economic or business risks assumed by the taxpayer, 3) the substance of an act or transaction hides the true will of the parties.

In the abovementioned circumstances DIAN may re-characterize or reconfigure any transaction or series of transactions by establishing its true nature and ignoring the effects of the artificial ones. Furthermore, DIAN is entitled to issue a new assessment of the taxes, interests and sanctions.

I.3.2. Thin Capitalization Rules

Thin capitalization rules are applicable in Colombia since 2013 (article 118-1 TS). Interest expenses can only be deducted if they are derived from indebtedness and the average value of debt does not exceed three times the entity's net equity. A ratio 4 to 1 is in place for special purpose companies, entities or vehicles whose purpose is the construction of social housing. The equity taken into account is the taxpayer's net equity for the preceding year, and the debt taken into account is debt that accrues interest.

Thin cap rules are not applicable to interests generated in credits granted by companies under the surveillance of the Financial Superintendence of Colombia or foreign entities under the surveillance of the authority watching the financial system provided that the Taxpayer meet certain conditions (article 118-1 TS). These, however, neither apply to credits granted by foreign associated enterprises as defined by the transfer pricing regime, nor to credits granted by entities located in non-cooperative jurisdictions (article 118-1 TS).

I.3.3. CFC Legislation

Colombia introduced CFC rules in 2016. CFCs are defined as corporations and investment vehicles –e.g. trusts, collective-investment funds, and private interest foundations-, meeting the conditions to be considered a related party for transfer pricing purposes. The CFC regime applies to residents (including corporations and entities) that directly or indirectly hold an interest equal to, or greater than 10% of the capital or of the profits of a foreign entity considered as a CFC.

According to the CFC rules, taxpayers subject to the CIT should not wait to receive a distribution of profits in Colombia to recognize the net profits of the CFC derived from passive income, in proportion to their participation in the CFC's capital or profits.

For CFC purposes, the following proceeds are considered as passive income: 1) Dividend and profit distributions from a company or investment vehicle, 2) Interest, 3) Income derived from the exploitation of intangibles, 4) Income from the sale of assets that generates passive income, 5) Income from the sale or lease of immovable property, 6) Income derived from the sale or purchase of tangible goods acquired from (or sold to) a related party if the manufacturing and consumption of the goods occurs in a jurisdiction different from the one in which the CFC is located or is tax resident, 7) Income from the performance of certain services in a jurisdiction different to the one of residence or location of the CFC.

It is important to note that whenever the dividends and benefits distributed by a CFC have been already taxed in Colombia, the income should be considered non-taxable for the Colombian taxpayer.

A tax credit is allowed for taxes paid abroad with respect to the passive income whenever the Colombian tax resident recognizes taxable income under the application of the CFC rules.

I.4. Tax Treaty Law

Colombia started negotiating Conventions for the Avoidance of Double Taxation in the seventies. At that time treaties were related to income for shipping and air companies and were negotiated with Germany, Argentina, Brazil, France, Italy, Panamá, Venezuela and the United States of America. The negotiation of Double Taxation Conventions on Income (DTC) started in 2005 with the tax treaty with Spain. Thenafter other treaties negotiated include DTCs with Chile, South Korea, Canada, India, México, Portugal, Czech Republic, and Switzerland.

The tax treaty network is limited and the country lacks DTCs with some of its main trading partners, *e.g.* United States and Venezuela. For a number of years the shortage of tax treaties was compensated with diverse tax incentives to attract foreign investment, domestic measures to avoid double taxation and the so called contracts for legal stability. These agreements between the State and individuals/entities were intended to freeze new tax law regimes or interpretations making the tax situation adverse for the taxpayer, over a period of 20 years. The taxpayer could apply new provisions beneficial to him. As from 2013 such agreements are no longer available. Other agreements for the mutual promotion and protection of investments expressly excluded tax provisions from its scope (*e.g.* the treaty with Spain, 2005).

In addition to the DTC, Colombia ratified the Multilateral Convention on Mutual Administrative Assistance in Tax Matters in 2013 and became member of the OECD Global Forum on Transparency and Exchange of Information for Tax Purposes in 2015, getting the approval of phases 1 and 2 re exchange of information. Furthermore, in 2014 entered in force the Tax Information Exchange Agreement (TIEA) between the

USA and Colombia. Colombia also signed a bilateral agreement for mutual assistance with Venezuela (1998) as well as a TIEA between the Republic of Colombia and the Kingdom of the Netherlands in respect of Curaçao (2012). The later agreement however does not seem to be in force. The text of majority of the tax treaties can be reached online[5].

I.4.1. Adherence to UN or OECD MC

Although Colombia is in the process of accession to the OECD, Double Taxation Conventions do not always follow the OECD Model Tax Convention and tend to rely more on the UN Model. Important deviations of the OECD Model regard, *e.g.*: (a) allocation rules, (b) scope and definitions of business profits, Permanent Establishments and royalties. Colombian DTCs do not define services for treaty purposes and this may collide with internal definitions of technical assistance, technical services and the understanding of intangibles such as know-how. In general, treaties do incorporate rules regarding anti-treaty shopping.

I.4.2. Special Features commonly present on Tax Treaties

Colombia classifies as a dualist state requiring all treaties to be incorporated before they can have any domestic legal effects. Furthermore, for the treaty to enter in force a control of compliance with the Constitution by the Constitutional Court is required. Treaty override is not common in Colombia.

---

5 See http://www.dian.gov.co/contenidos/normas/convenios.html

1.4.2.1 Scope of the tax treaties

Double Taxation Conventions on Income			
	Scope		
Country	Income and supplementary (capital gains) tax	CREE	Wealth (*Patrimonio / Riqueza*)
Canada	X	X	X
Chile	X	X	X
Corea	X	X	
España	X	X	X
Francia	X	X	X *
India	X	X	
México	X	X	X
Portugal	X	X	
Czech Republic	X	X	
Suiza	X	X	X
	* Only applicable if both countries derive the tax in the same taxable year		

Transport tax treaties				
	taxes covered			
Country	Income and supplementary (capital gains) tax	Solidarity income tax CREE	Wealth *Patrimonio / Riqueza*	Trade tax *ICA*
Germany	X	X	X	X
Argentina	X	X		X

Brazil	X	X	X	X
Italy	X	X	X	X
Panama	X	X	X	
Venezuela	X	X	X	
United States	X	X		X

1.4.2.2 Variations in the definition of permanent establishments

	Chile	México	Canada	Spain	Switzer-land	India	Czech Republic	Portugal	Korea	France
	2007	2009	2008	2005	2007	2011	2012	2010	2010	2015
Building site/project	X	X	X	X	X	X	X	X	X	X
Construction project	X	X	X	X	X	X	X	X	X	X
Installation project	X	X	X	X	X	X	X	X	X	X
Assembly project		X	X	X		X	X	X		X
Preparatory Work / on site planning*			X				X*		X	
Supervisory activities in connection therewith	X	X	X	X		X	X	X	X	X
Furnishing of services	X	X	X			X	X	X		X
Consultancy services	X	X	X			X	X	X		X
Individuals PE		X								
Computing the time limits between associated enterprises, if the activities of both enterprises are identical or substantially similar. * same project*	X		X						X	X*
Time limits										
12 months										
6 months	X	X	X	X	X	X	X	X	X	
183 days										X

1.4.2.3 Variations in regard dividends

	Taxed dividends		no taxed dividends
	General Rule (art. 10(2)(b))	Special rule for companies (art. 10(2)(a))	
Canada	15%	5% when the beneficial owner is a company which holds directly or indirectly at least 10% of the shares with right to vote of the company paying the dividends	15%
Chile	7%	0% when the beneficial owner is a company which holds directly at least 25 per cent of the capital of the company paying the dividends.	**General rule:** 0% if owns at least 25% and 7% for all other cases **Special rule** 38.25% or 7%*
Korea	10%	5% when the beneficial owner is a company, partnerships excluded, which holds directly at least 20 per cent of the capital of the company paying the dividends.	15%

Spain	5%	0% when the beneficial owner is a company which holds directly or indirectly at least 20% of the capital of the company paying the dividends.	**General rule:** 0% if owns at least 25% and 5% for all other cases
			Special rule 38.25% or 5%*
India	5%		15%
Mexico	0%		33%
Portugal	10%		33%
Czech Republic	15%	5% when the beneficial owner is a company, partnerships excluded, which holds directly at least 25 per cent of the capital of the company paying the dividends.	25%
Switzerland	15%	0% when the beneficial owner is a company which holds directly or indirectly at least 20% of the capital of the company paying the dividends.	This DTC does not make any difference between taxed and not taxed dividends

1.4.2.4 Withholding rates applicable under tax treaties

	Dividends	Interest	Royalties
Canada	5/15	5/10	10
Chile	0/7/35	5/15	10

Czech Republic	5/15/25	0/10	10
India	5/15	0/5/10	10
Korea (South)	5/10/15	0/5/10	10
Mexico	0/33	5/10	10
Portugal	10/33	0/10	10
Spain	0/5/35	0/5/10	10
Switzerland	0/15	0/5/10	10

I.4.3. Treaties Currently in Force

The following treaties are in force in Colombia:

- DTC related to income for shipping and air companies, above mentioned.
- The DTCs with Canada, Chile, the Czech Republic, India, Korea (South), Mexico, Portugal, Spain and Switzerland are in force. The treaties with France and the United Kingdom are not yet applicable.
- The Multilateral Convention on Mutual Administrative Assistance in Tax Matters
- The Tax Information Exchange Agreement (TIEA) between the USA and Colombia.
- The bilateral agreement for mutual assistance with Venezuela (1998).
- The intergovernmental agreement (IGA) for the implementation of the Foreign Account Tax Compliance Act (FATCA) with the USA.

I.5. Community Law

I.5.1. Participation in a Community/Union

Colombia is a member of the Andean Community (AC), former Andean Pact. Current Member Countries include Bolivia, Colombia, Ecuador and Peru. The authorities of the Andean Community include the Court of Justice (ACJ) and the Parliament. The ACJ has issued a number of judgments concerning the interpretations and applications of the tax measures adopted by the Community in the so call "Decisiones" (hereinafter Directives), stating the rules applicable to the income tax in cross border transactions between the AC Member Countries.

I.5.2. Rules regarding Corporate Income Taxation within the Andean Community

Directives 40 and 578 govern the CIT at the AC level. The Directive 578 of the Committee of the Cartagena Agreement provides the grounds for the taxation of intra community payments within the AC, whereas Annex II of the Decision 40 governs the relations between Member States and third Countries.

AC law relies on source as the criterion to establish the country with the right to tax the income. The Directive 578, article 3, states that all kinds of income are taxable by the Member State in which the income was generated ("fuente productora"), with few exceptions, for instance profits derived by transportation enterprises and for capital gains from ships, aircrafts, buses and other means of transportation, as well as commercial papers, shares and other securities[6]. Other member countries are expected to apply the exemption method. This also applies in the case of income from services and royalties. All income taxed in other Andean countries (having its source therein) should be considered exempt in Colombia. According to the TS, expenses incurred to obtain such exempt income are not deductible.

The "fuente productora" is not necessarily related to the place of payment, nor to the performance-taking place from a specific country. Instead, the decision refers it to: 1) the place where the activity takes place if business profits are involved, 2) the place where an intangible is used or the place where the right to use an intangible is enjoyed, 3) the place where a service is performed when dealing with personal services, 4) income derived by enterprises of professional services, technical services, technical assistance and consulting services are taxable only by the member country in whose territory the benefit of such services takes place. Unless it is proven otherwise, the Decision presumes that in the latter case the benefit takes place where the expense is imputed and recorded. (the payer's country).

A closer look to the DTCs signed by AC Member States indicate that whilst the tax treaty policy adopted by AC law to rule the relation of its Members with third countries did not play a role, the one intended for the internal market works well.

The main features for the taxation of passive income and the taxation of services in the AC Member Countries are as follows:

---

6   AC Decisión 578, "Régimen para evitar la doble tributación y prevenir la evasión fiscal," may 4, 2004, Official Journal n° 1063, available at http://www.comunidadandina.org, article 3, last accessed on 1 August 2016.

	Colombia		Bolivia	Ecuador	Peru
Dividends	5% Exempt for compa-nies taxed on individu-als 38,25%	– Dividends paid to for-eign com-panies or entities without domicile in Colombia, if the profits that are paid as divi-dends were taxed at the corporate level – Dividends paid to res-idents from profits taxed at the level of the Company. – Other cases.	25% over 50% of the dividends from Boli-vian origin (effective tax rate 12,5%)	0% – 35%	5%
Interests	15%	– General rule	25% over 50% of the dividends from Boli-vian origin (effective tax rate 12,5%)	22% 0% (to interna-tional pri-vate finan-cial insti-tutions)	4,99% 30%
Royalties	15%	– General – Soft-ware – Movies	25% over 50% of the dividends from Boli-vian origin (effective tax rate 12,5%)	22%	30%

Services rendered in Colombia	15%				
Technical Services	15% 0%	There is no withholding tax for technical services rendered from free zones.	25% over 50% of the dividends from Bolivian origin (effective tax rate 12,5%)	22%	30% 15% 0%
Tax holidays	35%			35% (if the payment is received by a resident) 25% (advances on dividends) 13% (dividends distributed to companies and trusts)	30% (for interest)

I.5.2.1. Dividends

AC law does not define dividends, hence domestic definitions apply. For AC purposes dividends are taxed in the country wherein the company making the distribution has its domicile whereas they are not taxable in the member country where the dividends are received by the receiving company or investor, or upon distribution to the shareholders (article 10)[7].

---

[7] In this vein see , DIAN Concept 44634 of May 6, 2008.

I.5.2.2. Interest

Interest and other financial interests are taxable in the Member Country where the payment is imputed and recorded, in other terms, the member state where the debtor is located has the right to tax. For instance, in application of this allocation rule DIAN concluded that interests received by a Colombian company from a person located in another member state will be treated as except income (Concept 32229 of May 18, 2002). Interest is defined for AC purposes as income of any nature, including financial returns on loans, deposits and fund raising made by private financial institutions, with or without a mortgage guarantee, or the right to participate in the debtor's profits, income from public funds (bonds issued by public entities) and bonds or obligations, including premiums and prizes related to such securities. Default penalties are not considered interest.

I.5.2.3. Royalties

Under Directives 578 and 40, AC Member States are obliged to tax royalty payments on a source basis. Apart from that, subject to the provisions of AC law, the Member States are competent to define the tax regime applicable to intangible technological contributions that are not capital contributions. The level of taxation varies depending on the country, but there is no possibility for tax exemption of royalty payments. The effective income tax rates for royalty payments range between 12.5% and 33% depending on the country.

One of the most controversial issues concerning AC law regards the allocation rule of royalty payments in the old conflict source vs residence[8]. This topic has not suffered any change under the Directive 578,[9] compared to the Directive 40. It seems that AC law followed the recommendation made by legal scholars in the session of the ILADT in Montevideo in 1996, proposing to follow taxation at source in every integration zone,[10] in order to avoid distortions, eliminate double taxation and simplify the tax systems.[11] A similar criterion was proposed by the Latina American Institute of Tax Law (ILADT) for its Model Tax Convention in 2010[12].

Annex II of Decision 40 rules the relations between AC Member States and third countries. In this case, AC Member States shall also follow the principle of taxation at source.[13] It applies to payments of royalties, services, professional services and technical assistance.[14]

---

[8]   Criticism regards the repetition of domestic law. In practice AC Member States started negotiating DTCs with third countries quiet lately. Furthermore, basically none followed the AC Model for negotiation with third states.

[9]   Decisión 578, Régimen para evitar la doble tributación y prevenir la evasión fiscal, en: Gaceta Oficial del Acuerdo de Cartagena, n°. 1063, 2004 http://www.comunidadandina.org/normativa/dec/D578.htm, article 9, last accessed on 1 August 2016.

[10] The most known in Latin America are CARICOM, MERCOSUR and the Andean Community.

[11] The Recommendation is available at: http://www.iladt.org/documentos/ detalle_doc.asp?id=380, 3rd recommendation, last accessed on 1 August 2017.

[12] Article 9 Model Tax Convention for Latin America, as presented in the "XXV Jornadas Latinoamericanas de Derecho Tributario", Cartagena de Indias, February, 2010.

[13] In the so called «producing source», see, Decisión 40: Aprobación del Convenio para evitar la doble tributación entre los Países Miembros y del Convenio Tipo para la celebración de acuerdos sobre doble tributación entre los Países Miembros y otros Estados ajenos a la Subregión, November 8 to 16, 1971, available at http://www.comunidadandina.org, last accessed on 1 August 2017.

[14] According to the MC approved by the Decision 40, ibid.

I.5.3. Jurisprudence regarding Corporate Income Taxation within the Andean Community

The Andean Court of Justice (ACJ) has issued a number of decisions on cases related to the application of Andean Community (AC) law. Some of the most relevant are:

I.5.3.1. Business profits

In application of article 7 of the Directive 40, in connection with article 4 of its annex I, the ACJ stated that any kind of income is taxable in the country in which they are obtained irrespective of the domicile or nationality of the person who obtains it. As to the Court this as a consequence of the source taxation principle in force in the AC[15].

I.5.3.2. Services, technical services, technical assistance and consultancy

In application of article 14 of the Directive 578, the ACJ concluded that profits related to services, technical services, technical assistance and consultancy are taxed in the country where the payment is booked and registered, considering this as the country where the benefit of the services takes place. The Court points this is an exception to the source tax principle governing AC law[16].

I.5.3.3. Dividends

In a request of prejudicial interpretation, the ACJ clarified that article 11 of the Directive 40 does not indicate whether dividends should have been booked or effectively paid. As to the ACJ this issue needs to be solved according to the domestic law of the Member States[17].

---

[15] ACJ, case 125-IP-2010.
[16] ACJ, case 37-IP-2011 y 63-IP-2011.
[17] ACJ, case 43-IP-2013.

I.5.3.4. Pensions

The ACJ concluded that in application of articles 8 and 9 of the Directive 583 (concerning Social security within the AC), related to the avoidance of double taxation of pensions, whenever a worker made its pension payments in its country of origin and also to the country in which he rendered services or worked, he is allowed to add the contributions made in the country of work to his country of origin. This approach would prevent losing the pension benefits or its decrease as a consequence of the migration[18].

I.5.3.5. Wealth tax

In a request of prejudicial interpretation of article 17 of the Directive 578, the ACJ concluded that such article involves a switch over clause given the purpose of the Directive to avoid double taxation and tax evasion. According to the Court the taxation of wealth (*patrimonio*) corresponds to the Member country in which such patrimony is located as long as that country taxes it. If that country does not tax it, the other Member state in which the taxable person is located could tax it if the wealth is subject to taxation therein[19].

I.5.3.6. Broadcasting Services

One of the landmark decisions taken in application of the Decision 40 by the State Council (SC), the maximum tribunal on tax matters in Colombia, regards the conclusion that payments derived from satellite broadcasting into Colombia are not of Colombian source and therefore not subject to a withholding tax in Colombia. The SC argued that payments made by the local operator to a foreign company are for a service related to the connection or access to

---

[18] ACJ, case 100-IP-2011.
[19] ACJ, cases 171-IP-2013, 184-IP-2013, 15-IP-2014, 230-IP-2013, 111-IP-2014.

the satellite located outside the national geostationary orbit. As to the SC, the income belongs to the country of domicile of the foreign broadcaster originating and sending the signal to the satellite. The SC believes that such a process takes place abroad and therefore it cannot be subject to withholding taxes in Colombia [20].

I.6. Influence of BEPS Action Plan on the Country

I.6.1. Adoption of rules in line with BEPS Reports

A number of provisions implement some actions of the BEPS reports:

I.6.1.1. Action 1

VAT is imposed on services rendered from abroad, at the place of use or consumption of the services as well as on the sale or license of intangibles related to industrial property.

I.6.1.2. Action 3

Colombia enacted CFC rules by law 1819, 2016.

I.6.1.3. Action 8, 9, 10

The transfer pricing regime includes now the Value creation criteria.

I.6.1.4. Action 13

Country by country reporting (as from 2016) concerning: 1) information related to the global allocation of revenues and taxes paid by MNE groups residents in Colombia with branches or subsidiaries abroad that are obliged to present

---

[20] SC, Judgment of July 12, 2007, fn. 15440.

consolidated financial statements and provided that their revenues are higher than aprox. COP2.4 billions, or 2) residents appointed as reporting entities by the foreign controlling entity.

Master file. Taxpayers are required to submit a master file with the relevant information of the multinational group, as well as a local file with the information related to each kind of transaction making evident the compliance with the transfer pricing rules.

The comparable uncontrolled price method is nowadays considered as the most appropriate method for raw materials and commodities.

In addition to the above, similar to the OECD approach, Colombian Tax Law no longer refers to the term tax havens, instead the term non-cooperative jurisdictions is in use. The law sets a number of criteria for the definition of such jurisdictions by future regulations.

I.6.2. Participation in Multilateral Instrument

Colombia is a signatory party of the MLI. DTC covered by the MLI include Canada, Chile, Czech Republic, Spain, France, India, Korea, Mexico, Portugal, Switzerland. Colombia introduced a number of reservations, the following amongst other:

- The right not to apply article 3 (transparent entities).
- Pursuant to Article 7(17)(a) of the Convention, whilst Colombia accepts the application of Article 7(1) alone as an interim measure, it intends where possible to adopt a limitation on benefits provision, in addition to or in replacement of Article 7(1), through bilateral negotiation.
- Pursuant to Article 7(17)(c) of the Convention, Colombia hereby chooses to apply the Simplified Limitation on Benefits Provision pursuant to Article 7(6).

- Pursuant to Article 10(5)(a) of the Convention, Colombia reserves the right for the entirety of Article 10 not to apply to its covered tax agreements the anti-abuse rule for permanent establishments situated in third jurisdictions.

I.7. Jurisprudence

Case law helps to illustrate that source rules are applied in an unexpected but quiet convenient way for foreign investment. A number of cases decided by the State Council between 2007 and 2015 concerning payments related to international television using satellites and communication to an automated database of a foreign company demonstrate this.

I.7.1. TV broadcasting services

In 2007, the SC addressed the issue of whether payments made to a foreign company for international television-broadcasting services into Colombia are subject to tax in Colombia. The SC did not uphold the characterization as royalties argued by the DIAN. Instead, the SC considered that payments for services are not subject to withholding tax in Colombia. In the SC view, the foreign broadcaster company and its local customer have different functions. The foreign company broadcast and rebroadcast the signal to a satellite. The local company connects to the satellite to get the signal in order to render the television service within Colombia. Therefore, payments to the foreign company are for the access to the satellite and not for rendering broadcasting services within Colombia.

According to the above mentioned, the fact that the foot print of the beam touches Colombia and the user of the signal is also located within the country are not enough reasons to sustain that the service is rendered in Colombia

[21]. As a consequence, and in application of articles 406, 12 and 24 TS, the income is not considered of Colombian source and it is not subject to withholding tax [22]. This Court decision repeats as a pattern in a number of similar cases until 2015[23].

I.7.2. Income from employment

Income derived by a foreign individual rendering services in Colombia is deemed to be of Colombian sources irrespective of the existence of an employment contract with a foreign Enterprise.

I.7.3. Communication services, databases

A Colombian company (X) made payments to companies in Spain (S) and Uruguay (U) for telecommunication services required for performing its own business activity of making tourist reservations. The services allowed X to access and work on an automated database owned by a German company. However, thetwo foreign companies had outsourced the supply of the telecom service to another Colombian company (TC) and hence were contractually required to instantly forward the payment received from X to TC. X did not apply WHT in Colombia, arguing that another Colombian company (TC) was the ultimate beneficiary of the payment, and hence no WHT was due. X claimed the payment could not be considered income in the hands of either S or U because it did not accrue to them.

---

21 SC, Judgments of June 14 2007, fn. 15686; October 10, 2007, fn. 15616, 15865, 15909, 15912.

22 SC, Judgements of August 2, 2007, refs. 15635, 15688, 15903,and February 2, 2008 ref. 16444. SC, decisions of October 3, 2007, ref. 15689. SC, decisions of October 10, 2007, refs. 15687, 15795, 15909.

23 SC, Judgements 020544 of 2015, 017795 of 2012, 018402 of 2012, 018561 of 2012, 017252 of 2011, 016616 of 09 016401 of 2009, 015787 of 2007, 015688 of 2007.

As to the SC, the failure to apply the WHT when required made the payment non-deductible. According to the Court: 1) the income was of domestic source and subject to WHT; 2) the payments were made to the foreign companies (S and U) as a consideration for the telecom service to enable the customers of the plaintiff (X) in Colombia to connect to the German database; (3) as such, the service is supplied within Colombia according to article 24 ITA; and 4) the beneficial ownership concept, or a possible reimbursement, argued by X was considered irrelevant for the application of the WHT[24].

1.8 Other taxes on business

As indicated previously, companies and entities doing business in Colombia may be subject to other direct taxes such as CREE, wealth tax and trade tax. The main features of these taxes are as follows:

Natural persons and companies involved in industrial activities, commercial activities and the provision of services.

	Solidarity tax (so called CREE, in force up to 2017)	Wealth tax	Trade tax
Taxable event	Income that may likely increase the patrimony of taxpayers in the taxable year.	The wealth tax is generated by the possession of wealth, whose value is equal to or greater than $1,000 million pesos.	Industrial activities, commercial activities and services.

---

24 SC judgment, of 11 December 2008, fn. 15968.

Taxpayers	National taxpayers whether individuals or legal entities. Companies and foreign entities taxpayers of the income tax on their income from national sources, obtained through branches and/or PEs in Colombia.	Legal entities, individuals and illiquid succession who are taxpayers of the income tax. —— Companies and foreign entities taxpayers of the income tax on their income from national sources, obtained through branches and/or permanent	Natural persons and companies involved in industrial activities, commercial activities and the provision of services.
Taxable Base	Gross income minus returns, rebates and discounts results in net income. 　　Net income minus costs incurred in the generation of net income and deductions results in the taxable income.	Wealth of the person (For purposes of this tax, the concept of wealth is equivalent to the total gross assets of the taxpayer minus debts)	Annual gross income

Rate	9% general tax rate ———— A surcharge exists when the taxable base is equal or higher than $800 million pesos. For 2015 was of 5%, 2016 is of 6%, 2017 and 2018 will be of 8% and 9% respectively.	The rates for the wealth tax are shown below.	2-7 X 1000 for industrial activities ———— 2-10 X 1000 for commercial activities and services

Legal Persons Wealth tax for the year 2016			
Taxable base range		Marginal tax rate	Tax
Lower limit	Upper limit		
>0	<2.000.000.000	0.15%	(taxable Base) * 0,15%
>=2.000.000.000	<3.000.000.000	0.25%	((taxable Base – $ 2.000.000.000) * 0.25%) + $ 3.000.000
>=3.000.000.000	<5.000.000.000	0,50%	((taxable Base – $ 3.000.000.000) * 0.50%) + $ 5.500.000
>=5.000.000.000	Onwards	1.00%	((taxable Base – $ 5.000.000.000) * 1.00%) + $ 15.500.000

Legal Persons Wealth tax for the year 2017			
Taxable base range		Marginal tax rate	Tax
Lower limit	Upper limit		
>0	<2.000.000.000	0.05%	(taxable Base) * 0,05%
>=2.000.000.000	<3.000.000.000	0.10%	((taxable Base − $ 2.000.000.000) * 0,10%) + $ 1.000.000
>=3.000.000.000	<5.000.000.000	0.20%	((taxable Base − $ 3.000.000.000) * 0.20%) + $ 2.000.000
>=5.000.000.000	Onwards	0.40%	((taxable Base − $ 5.000.000.000) * 0.40%) + $ 6.000.000

Natural Persons Wealth tax for the year 2015, 2016, 2017 and 2018			
Taxable base range		Marginal tax rate	Tax
Lower limit	Upper limit		
>0	<2.000.000.000	0.125%	(taxable Base) * 0,125%
>=2.000.000.000	<3.000.000.000	0.35%	((taxable Base − $ 2.000.000.000) * 0.35%) + $2.500.000

>=3.000.000.000	<5.000.000.000	0.75%	((taxable Base – $ 3.000.000.000) * 0.75%) + $ 6.000.000
>=5.000.000.000	Onwards	1.15%	((taxable Base – $ 5.000.000.000) * 1.15%) + $ 21.000.000

5

Mexico

Mrs. Ana Paula Pardo • Mr. Jorge San Martín Elizondo

I.1. Corporate Income Tax at Domestic level

Under the Income Tax Law, Mexican resident legal entities
are subject to income tax on a worldwide basis. That is, they
are required to pay income tax in Mexico with respect to
the totality of income they receive, regardless of the source
from which it may derive.

Since Mexican resident legal entities are bound to pay
income tax over the totality of their income, irrespective
of its source, it is important to address the concept of
residency. Accordingly, a legal entity could be deemed as
a Mexican resident when their business' headquarters or
their effective centre of management are established within
Mexican territory.

In contrast, foreign tax residents could be subject to
income taxation in Mexico regarding (i) any and all income
attributable to a permanent establishment of theirs set
up within Mexican territory; and/or (ii) Mexican-sourced
income received by them (that cannot be attributed to a
permanent establishment).

Generally speaking, a foreign tax resident could be
deemed to have a permanent establishment in Mexico when
business activities, whether in part or entirely, are carried out in Mexico or independent personal services are
rendered therein. Therefore, any branch, agency, office,
manufacturing facility, workshop, mine, or any other place

for the extraction, exploration or exploitation of natur-al resources, could be deemed to constitute a perma-nent establishment. Furthermore, a permanent establish-ment could also be deemed to exist if the foreign tax res-ident acts in Mexico by conduct of a dependent agent or an independent agent acting beyond its ordinary course of business.

Lastly, it is worth noting that the Income Tax Law provides the normative premises under which each income item received by a foreign resident could be considered as having its source in Mexico, hence triggering income tax therein.

I.1.1. Active Income

Considering that: (i) Mexican resident legal entities are liable for income tax on a worldwide basis; (ii) foreign res-idents are liable for income tax on income attributable to a permanent establishment of theirs set up within the coun-try; and/or (iii) for any income whose source is deemed to be located in Mexico (that cannot be attributed to a permanent establishment), the distinction between active and passive income would appear not to be as relevant at a domestic level.

Nonetheless, such distinction could be of vital impor-tance vis-à-vis the tax treatment applicable to specific transactions.

For instance, identifying an income item as business profits (an active income item) could be of paramount importance for foreign residents (without a permanent establishment within national territory). The foregoing giv-en that business profits could in some occasions be con-sidered not to have their source of income in Mexico and, as such, would not trigger income tax therein (in so far as such business profits are not subject to a preferential tax regime in the relevant entity's jurisdiction, in terms of the Income Tax Law. What is more, in terms of an administrative rule, certain income items could be deemed not to have their source of wealth in Mexico when the relevant transactions are conducted by independent parties or at fair market values).

Moreover, this distinction could be of relevance when deciding on the applicability of a particular tax regime (i.e., whether a trust should be considered as a business trust or not), or when it comes to deciding the applicable withholding tax for certain Mexican-sourced income items received by foreign residents.

I.1.1.1. Business Profits

Under Mexican law, business profits are considered as an active income item. For such purposes, business profits mean income obtained as consequence of the performance of commercial (as defined by the Code of Commerce), industrial, agricultural, stockbreeding and fishing activities.

In this regard, the Code of Commerce sets forth two general principles per which the character of commercial could be attributed to an activity. First, a subjective principle under which the following persons would be deemed as a (commercial) business: (i) individuals that have legal capacity to conduct business activities and do so as their occupation; (ii) business corporations incorporated in terms of Mexican commercial laws; and (iii) foreign corporations or agencies or branch offices thereof located within national territory that conduct business activities.

Secondly, an activity could be considered of a commercial nature in terms of an objective principle if it is one of the activities listed in article 75 of the Code of Commerce (article 75 consists of an extensive list of activities that are deemed as commercial activities). In view of the foregoing, the following, amongst others, could be identified as commercial activities: (a) the purchase and sale of immovable property when performed for speculation purposes; (b) transportation of people or goods by land or sea and tourism-related enterprises; (c) banking activities; (d) transactions involving securities in terms of the Negotiable Instruments and Credit Operations Law; or (e) insurance agreements of any sort.

I.1.1.1.1. Taxable Event

The recognition of an income item that could fall under any of the abovementioned categories, that is, commercial, industrial, agricultural, stockbreeding or fishing activities, by a taxable legal entity could trigger income tax on such business profits. Therefore, it is of paramount importance to identify the subject (taxpayer) receiving the relevant income for purposes of determining when income tax is triggered and how it should be calculated and paid.

Since Mexican resident companies are liable for income tax in Mexico on a worldwide basis, income items recognised by them as business profits would need to be added to the rest of their accruable income for the current tax year for purposes of determining the corresponding taxable basis.

When it comes to foreign residents, the tax treatment applicable in Mexico to business profits varies depending on whether it is attributable to a permanent establishment located in Mexico, or else, deemed as a Mexican-sourced income item.

In the first case, that is, when business profits are attributable to a permanent establishment set up in Mexico by a foreign resident, income tax would be triggered when income is derived by the permanent establishment and the foreign resident would be liable for the corresponding income tax as if it were a Mexican legal entity (a similar tax treatment applies).

Lastly, concerning foreign residents without a permanent establishment set up within national territory (or that even when having one, business profits cannot be attributed thereto), income tax would be triggered depending on the nature of the activities from which business profits are derived. Arguably, whilst certain business profits would not be considered as Mexican-sourced and as such would not be subject to income taxation in Mexico, other income items deemed as business profits could indeed be taxed therein (i.e. Mediation fees subject to a preferential tax regime in the creditor's jurisdiction could be considered as business profits subject to income tax in Mexico).

Without prejudice of the foregoing, under article 7 (Business Profits) of several of the double taxation agreements concluded by Mexico, business profits obtained by foreign residents (from jurisdictions with which such a treaty has been concluded) could be exempt from income tax in Mexico.

I.1.1.1.2. Taxable Basis

Mexican resident companies that receive business profits are required to accumulate them along with the rest of their accruable income generated during the corresponding tax year. Generally speaking, they would then subtract from their gross income allowed deductions (as set forth in the applicable tax laws), employees' profits sharing and pending losses from previous tax years, if any, for purposes of obtaining the taxable basis on which income tax ought to be paid.

It should be noted that whenever Mexican companies carry out activities from which business profits are derived by conduct of a business trust, then said trust would be required to determine income tax due by such entities and to comply with several formal tax obligations on behalf of them.

As per foreign residents with a permanent establishment located in Mexico, all income attributable thereto, including business profits, would be deemed as taxable income under the Income Tax Law. Since permanent establishments are given a similar treatment than that applicable to Mexican residents, foreign residents with a permanent establishment would also be required to determine their (gross) accruable income for the current tax year and could be allowed to reduce their taxable basis with specific deductions (i.e. in certain cases, expenses shared by permanent establishments of the foreign resident located in different jurisdictions could be deducted by the Mexican permanent establishment in the corresponding proportion).

Concerning taxable Mexican-sourced business profits obtained by a foreign resident (not attributable to a permanent establishment), the general rule would be for the taxable basis to be the gross amount of income received (business profits), without the possibility of claiming deductions.

Furthermore, when taxable income is received by a foreign resident acting through a Mexican trust, the latter would be required to determine income tax due on behalf of the first (consequently it would calculate the corresponding taxable basis) and to withhold the relevant amounts.

However, it should be noted that certain income items deemed as business profits received by foreign residents would not trigger income tax in terms of the Income Tax Law, or could even be exempted in terms of the applicable double taxation agreement concluded by Mexico and the country of which the relevant foreign resident is a tax resident.

I.1.1.1.3. Taxpayers

As per mentioned above, Mexican resident companies, foreign residents with a permanent establishment located in Mexico and in certain cases foreign residents without a permanent establishment in Mexico (or that even when having one the relevant income item cannot be attributed to), could be deemed as taxpayers as consequence of the attainment of business profits.

I.1.1.1.4. Tax rates

Mexican companies are taxed at the corporate rate of 30 per cent on taxable profits derived in the corresponding tax year.

Similarly, foreign tax residents with a permanent establishment within Mexican territory are required to accrue all income attributable thereto and to pay income tax thereupon (less allowed deductions, that is, on the taxable basis) at a 30 per cent tax rate.

In general terms, business profits received by foreign tax residents without a permanent establishment located in Mexico (or to which such business profits cannot be attributed) could be exempted from income tax in Mexico by means of a double taxation agreement.

Nonetheless, in cases where a Mexican-sourced income item received by foreign resident is deemed as taxable business profits, the applicable withholding tax rate could be of 40 per cent if such income item is considered as subject to a preferential tax regime in the country of which the creditor (the foreign resident) is a tax resident. The foregoing, in so far as the entities involved in the transaction are related parties and no tax information exchange agreement between Mexico and the corresponding jurisdiction is in force.

I.1.2. Passive Income

Hereunder you will find a comprehensive analysis with respect to the tax treatment to which income items traditionally characterised as passive income could be subject to under Mexican law. Accordingly, dividend, interest and royalty payments will be addressed with the purpose of outlining a general overview of the tax treatment applicable thereto.

I.1.2.1. Dividends

Pursuant to recent tax reforms implemented in Mexico and in effect as of 2014, the Mexican Income Tax Law adopted the form of a classic taxation system, that is, income tax is triggered: (i) when (taxable) profits are obtained; and (ii) whenever profits are distributed to the relevant shareholders (as explained further below certain exceptions apply).

In general terms, corporate entities are therefore liable for income tax due on profits derived during the relevant tax year and are required to withhold income tax whenever they distribute such profits or pay dividends to their shareholders (again, certain exceptions apply).

I.1.2.1.1. Taxable Event

Bearing in mind that, in principle, corporate entities are taxed on the profits they obtain in the corresponding tax year, (after-tax) net profits resulting from their activities are added to the relevant entity's after-tax earnings and profits account or "*Cuenta de Utilidad Fiscal Neta*" (commonly, and for purposes hereof, referred to as "CUFIN").

Dividends paid by a Mexican resident company are not subject to additional taxes on a corporate level in so far as they are paid out of their after-tax earnings and profits account or CUFIN since the balance of said account consists of distributable income which has already been subject to corporate taxation. However, should that not be the case (if dividends are not paid out of the CUFIN), the entity paying dividends would be required to pay the corresponding corporate tax at the time of the distribution.

In addition, and whether the distributable income is being paid out of the CUFIN or not (and therefore is subject to corporate taxation), an additional withholding tax would be triggered by the distribution of dividends if they are paid to foreign residents (legal entities or individuals) or Mexican individuals.

In light of the foregoing, foreign tax residents receiving dividends could trigger income tax in Mexico when said income item is deemed to be sourced in Mexico, that is, whenever the distributing entity is a Mexican company. In such cases, the Mexican company would be required to withhold income tax (regardless of the corporate tax paid at the time the corresponding profits were generated).

However, the aforesaid withholding tax would not be triggered if the dividends are paid by a Mexican resident company to another Mexican resident company. Instead, the amount distributed (paid) would be added and computed in the CUFIN of the recipient entity and subtracted from the CUFIN of the distributing entity.

I.1.2.1.2. Taxable Basis

As per mentioned above, whenever Mexican companies pay dividends out of their CUFIN, no additional corporate tax would be triggered. Nevertheless, in cases where dividends are not paid out of the CUFIN, corporate income tax (in addition to the withholding tax, if applicable) would be triggered.

Consequently, the distributing Mexican entity would be required to determine income tax due by multiplying the amount being paid (dividends) by 1.4286 and applying the corporate tax rate of 30 per cent to the result of the product.

It should be noted that the aforesaid mechanics or procedure would substantially vary in cases where the Mexican entity distributes profits (in terms of article 78 of the Income Tax Law) instead of properly paying dividends (i.e. reimbursements resulting from a capital reduction in a Mexican company could be treated as the distribution of profits).

With respect to foreign tax residents that receive taxable dividends from a Mexican company (deemed as Mexican-sourced), the taxable basis on which the withholding tax would be applied would be equal to the gross amount being paid (as dividends).

Furthermore, it should be noted that remittances paid by a permanent establishment in Mexico to its parent company abroad could also be subject to withholding on the gross amount being paid, since such payments would be deemed as dividends.

I.1.2.1.3. Taxpayers

As per mentioned above, taxation on profits and the distribution thereof in the form of dividends is twofold. Indeed, the taxpayers involved in such a transaction would be both the distributing entity (liable for the underlying corporate tax) and the recipient thereof as consequence of the applicable withholding tax, if any.

That is, the Mexican resident company paying dividends is deemed as a taxpayer with respect to the corporate tax due on the profits it obtains. Then, the recipients of the profits or dividends (i.e., the shareholders) are also deemed as taxpayers as consequence of the withholding tax in so far as they are foreign residents or Mexican individuals (considering that the tax effect regarding distributions between Mexican resident companies is reflected at the level of their respective CUFIN).

Moreover, foreign tax residents could be deemed as taxpayers when a permanent establishment of theirs sends remittances to its parent company abroad.

I.1.2.1.4. Tax rates

Currently, the corporate tax to which Mexican resident companies are subject to is of 30 per cent. Consequently, whenever a Mexican resident company pays dividends that have not been subject to corporate taxation (not from their CUFIN), the corporate tax applicable thereto would be the result of applying the 30 per cent rate to the amount distributed multiplied by 1.4286.

It is worth noting, however, that (assuming certain requirements are met) corporate income tax paid (30 per cent) at the level of the distributing Mexican company could be credited by the recipient of the dividends against income tax on future profits in the current tax year or in the following two tax years.

Regarding dividends paid by a Mexican resident company to foreign residents (legal entities or individuals), as well as to Mexican resident individuals, the additional withholding tax would be determined by applying a 10 per cent tax rate to the gross amount being distributed.

In some cases, in addition to the applicable withholding tax, Mexican individuals that receive dividends could have an additional tax burden of up to 5 per cent, depending on their applicable progressive tax rate (since they are subject to income tax on the totality of income they receive at a rate of up to 35 per cent and are only allowed to credit the corporate tax paid by the distributing entity at a rate of 30 per cent).

Notwithstanding the abovementioned tax treatment under Mexican laws, relief in the form of reduced tax rates or even exemptions could be provided by means of a double taxation agreement concluded by Mexico and the country of which the (foreign) recipient is a tax resident.

I.1.2.2. Interest

Pursuant to the Income Tax Law, the term *interest* applies to yields on credits of any kind, regardless of the name used or given thereto. Amongst others, the following items are considered as forms of interest: yields on public debt, on bond or debentures, including discounts and premiums; premiums on repurchase agreements or securities lending;

commissions charged for opening or guaranteeing credits; considerations for accepting joint liabilities or granting a guarantee or a liability of any kind, except when said considerations must be paid to insurance and bonding institutions; gains on the sale of bonds, securities and other negotiable instruments, provided that they are of the type that are placed among the general investing public in accordance with the general rules issued for said purposes by the tax authorities.

Generally speaking, interest payments are accruable income for the recipient and a deductible expense for the payer, provided that certain requirements are met. It should be kept in mind that the term *payment* includes any form under which the obligation to pay the interest is extinguished.

Amongst the conditions that ought to be met for interests to be deductible for income tax purposes the following, *inter alia*, can be found:

1. Interest payments (expense) must be strictly necessary for the performance of the taxpayer's activity.
2. Where applicable, income tax due on interest payments must be effectively withheld for the relevant payment to be deemed as deductible.
3. The loan must be duly recorded with proper documentation supporting the transaction (agreements, notes, wire transfer, checks, bank account statements).
4. The loan must be duly registered in the relevant entity's accounting records.
5. Concerning transactions between related parties, the arm's length principle must be abided by (fair market values);
6. Other formal obligations such as the filing of informative tax returns regarding payments realised abroad, identifying related parties, amongst others; and
7. Thin capitalisation rules must be abided by.

8. Interest payments made in favour of a foreign legal entity that controls or is controlled by the taxpayer making the corresponding payments would not be deductible if any of the following conditions are met (certain exceptions could apply):

    a. The foreign legal entity that receives interest income is fiscally transparent, unless the shareholders or beneficiaries thereof are actually subject to income tax on income derived from said legal entity and the payment made by the (Mexican) taxpayer abides by the arm's-length principle (in which case interest payments could be deducted);

    b. The relevant payment is deemed as inexistent (for tax purposes) in the country or jurisdiction where the foreign legal entity is located; or

    c. The foreign legal entity is not bound to recognise such payment as taxable income under the laws applicable thereto.

I.1.2.2.1. Taxable Event

Mexican resident corporations are subject to income tax on a worldwide basis. Bearing this in mind, income received as interest payments ought to be accrued with the rest of income items received by the relevant Mexican entity during the current tax year.

Likewise, interest payments received by a foreign resident with a permanent establishment status from a Mexican company would be deemed as income attributable to the permanent establishment and as such, as taxable income. In such cases, the foreign resident with the permanent establishment status would also be required to accrue said interest payments with the rest of income items attributable to the permanent establishment in order to determine income tax due in the current tax year.

Concerning interest payments received by a foreign resident (without a permanent establishment set up within the country or to which interest payments cannot be attributed to), income deriving therefrom would be deemed as sourced in Mexico if the capital or principal on which such interests are being accrued is invested within the country or when the debtor (the entity paying interests) is a Mexican resident or a foreign resident with a permanent establishment in Mexico.

Accordingly, interest payments received by a foreign resident that are considered as Mexican-sourced could be subject to taxation in Mexico.

Interests paid by a Mexican resident to a foreign resident without a permanent establishment within national territory are deemed to have a Mexican source of wealth. In accordance with the Income Tax Law, in such cases, the payer would be required to withhold the corresponding tax (the applicable rate may vary depending on several factors including the nature of the parties involved, nonetheless the top rate is 35%) when such interests become due or are paid, whatever happens first.

I.1.2.2.2. Taxable Basis

Mexican companies ought to add interest payments with the rest of accruable income received during the current tax year. Their taxable basis would then be determined by subtracting allowed deductions, employee's profit sharing and pending losses from previous tax years, if any, from gross income received during the corresponding tax year.

Interest payments received by a foreign resident's permanent establishment located within Mexican territory would be deemed as accruable income. Therefore, the taxable basis on which the permanent establishment would be required to pay income tax could be its net profits (gross income, less allowed deductions) for the relevant tax year.

However, in cases where interest payments regarding the permanent establishment located in Mexico are made to the parent company or another permanent establishment thereof, the Mexican permanent establishment would be bound to make the corresponding withholding within the following 15 days after that in which the interest payment is made or the (Mexican permanent establishment) deducts such expense, whatever happens first.

Generally speaking, the taxable basis on which foreign tax residents that receive taxable interest payments (Mexican-sourced) from a Mexican company or a foreign resident's permanent establishment located in Mexico would be required to pay income tax, would be equal to the gross amount being paid (without the possibility of claiming deductions)

I.1.2.2.3. Taxpayers

As per mentioned above, under the applicable Mexican laws, Mexican resident companies, foreign residents' permanent establishments located in Mexico and foreign residents (receiving Mexican-sourced income) could be deemed as taxpayers with respect to interest payments.

I.1.2.2.4. Tax rates

Mexican resident companies receiving interest payments are subject to the corporate tax rate of 30 per cent (applied to the taxable basis determined for the corresponding tax year).

Similarly, foreign residents with a permanent establishment located in Mexico would be bound to accrue the totality of income they perceive, amongst which interest payments could be found, and to pay income tax at the corporate rate of 30 per cent on their taxable basis (gross income, less allowed deductions).

Lastly, the tax rate to which foreign tax residents receiving Mexican-sourced interest payments could be subject to ranges from 4.9 to 35 per cent, depending on the nature of the creditor and the debtor or the concept for which such interests are being paid. Nonetheless, a withholding tax rate of 40 per cent could result applicable if income received by the foreign tax resident is deemed to be subject to a preferential tax regime (according to Mexican laws) and the applicable provisions are not complied with.

Despite the foregoing, interests due or paid to a foreign resident could benefit from reduced withholding rates set forth in a double taxation agreement to which Mexico is part (i.e. withholding tax rates of 5%, 10% or 15%).

I.1.1.3. Royalties

In general terms, royalties and technical assistance paid by a Mexican resident to a foreign resident are subject to income tax in Mexico. However, it is important to define the concepts for which such payments are made, given that tax treatment corresponding to royalties or technical assistance could greatly vary, both for purposes of the Income Tax Law and the applicable double taxation agreements. In fact, whereas the payment of royalties could be subject to a withholding tax, the payment of technical assistance could be exempt from income tax in Mexico pursuant to the tax treatment set forth in double taxation agreements.

For such purposes, the term *royalties* under Mexican Law (Article 15-B of the Federal Fiscal Code) includes payments of any kind for the temporary use or enjoyment of patents; certificates of invention or improvement; trademarks, trade names; copyrights of literary, artistic or scientific works, including motion pictures and recordings for radio or television, as well as of drawings or models, blueprints, formulas, procedures, industrial, commercial or scientific equipment, and amounts paid for technology transfers or information regarding industrial, commercial or scientific experiences, or other, similar rights or property. Furthermore, the consideration paid for the transfer of patrimonial rights could also be deemed as royalty payments.

Moreover, pursuant to Article 12 of the OECD's Model Tax Convention on Income and on Capital, royalties means: " [...] *payments of any kind received as a consideration for the use of, or the right to use, any copyright of literary, artistic or scientific work including cinematograph films, any patent, trade mark, design or model, plan, secret formula or process, or for information concerning industrial, commercial or scientific experience.*"

From the preceding definition, please note that the term *royalties* includes payments for the use of information concerning industrial, commercial, or scientific experience (commonly known as *know-how*). Therefore, payments as consideration for know-how would also fall under the scope of Article 12, and would therefore be treated as royalties.

What is more, royalties paid to a foreign related party could be fully deductible for income tax purposes, provided that the benefit derived thereof is realised in the same year in which the deduction is claimed. Otherwise, they may be depreciated annually, under the straight-line method at the 15% rate.

In addition, for royalty payments to be deductible other requirements should be met, amongst which the following (essential requirements) can be found:

1) Royalties must be strictly necessary for the taxpayer's activity;

2) The arm's length principle must be abided by; and

3) Income tax withholdings must be performed (for which a tax residency certificate of the beneficiary for each year should be obtained).

On the other hand, from a Mexican legal standpoint, technical assistance and technical services mean the rendering of independent personal services for which the service provider undertakes to provide non-patentable knowledge that does not entail the transfer of confidential information on industrial, trade or scientific experiences and under-takes with the provider to intervene in implementing said knowledge.

In this regard, Commentary 11.3 of the OECD's Model Tax Convention on Income and on Capital, establishes that the following criteria could be relevant to distinguish royalty and technical assistance payments:

- Contracts for the supply of know-how (royalties) concern information that already exists that has not been patented and does not generally fall within other categories of intellectual property rights. It generally corresponds to un-divulged information of an industrial, commercial or scientific nature arising from previous experience, which has practical application in the operation of an enterprise and from the disclosure of which an economic benefit can be derived or concern the supply of that type of information after its development or creation and include specific provisions concerning the confidentiality of that information.

- In the case of contracts for the provision of services (technical assistance), the supplier undertakes to perform services which may require the use, by that supplier, of special knowledge, skill and expertise but not the transfer of such special knowledge, skill or expertise to the other party.

- In most cases involving the supply of know-how, there would generally be very little more which needs to be done by the supplier under the contract other than to supply existing information or reproduce existing material. On the other hand, a contract for the performance of services would, in most cases, involve a very much greater level of expenditure by the supplier in order to perform his contractual obligations. For instance, the supplier, depending on the nature of the services to be rendered, may have to incur salaries and wages for employees engaged in researching, designing, testing, drawing and other associated activities or payments to sub-contractors for the performance of similar services.

In light of the foregoing, pursuant to Commentary 11.4. of the OECD's Model Tax Convention on Income and on Capital, the following payments should not be considered as consideration for the provision of know-how but, rather, for the provision of services:

- payments obtained as consideration for after-sales service;
- payments for services rendered by a seller to the purchaser under a warranty;
- payments for pure technical assistance;
- payments for an opinion given by an engineer, an advocate or an accountant, and payments for advice provided electronically, for electronic communications with technicians or for accessing, through computer networks, a trouble-shooting database such as a database that provides users of software with non-confidential information in response to frequently asked questions or common problems that arise frequently.

I.1.2.3.1. Taxable Event

As was the case of other income items, income tax would be triggered whenever a Mexican company receives royalty payments (since they are taxed on a worldwide basis).

Likewise, royalty payments attributable to a foreign resident's permanent establishment located within Mexican territory would be considered as taxable income in Mexico.

Lastly, concerning foreign tax residents that receive royalty payments, income tax would be triggered in Mexico in so far as such payments are sourced in Mexico. In this regard, the Income Tax Law provides that income deriving from royalties (as well as technical assistance or advertising), could be deemed as Mexican-sourced when the assets or rights for which the royalties (or the technical assistance) are paid are exploited in Mexico; or whenever royalties (or technical assistance fees or the advertising fees) are paid by a Mexican resident or by a foreign resident with a permanent establishment set up in Mexican territory.

I.1.2.3.2. Taxable Basis

Mexican companies that receive royalty payments would be required to accumulate such income item with the rest of their accruable income. The corresponding taxable basis would then be determined by subtracting allowed deductions, employee's profit sharing and pending losses from previous tax years, if any, from their gross income.

Concerning foreign residents with a permanent establishment located set up in Mexico, royalty payments attributable thereto would also be deemed as accruable income. Therefore, their taxable basis would be equal to the result of subtracting allowed deductions from the gross income attributed to the permanent establishment during the relevant tax year.

However, it should be noted that whenever royalty payments (in connection with foreign residents with a permanent establishment in Mexico) are made by the parent company or by a permanent establishment thereof set up in a different jurisdiction, income tax due would need to be withheld by the Mexican permanent establishment within the following 15 days after that in which the corresponding payment is made or when the Mexican permanent establishment deducts such expense, whatever happens first. The applicable withholding tax rate would need to be applied to the gross amount of the consideration.

Finally, the applicable taxable basis for foreign tax residents receiving royalty payments sourced in Mexico would be equal to the gross amount of the consideration (royalty payments), without the possibility of claiming any deduction.

I.1.2.3.3. Taxpayers

As has been the case throughout this chapter, Mexican companies, foreign tax residents with a permanent establishment set up within Mexican territory and foreign residents with Mexican-sourced income that receive royalty payments could be deemed as taxpayers under the Income Tax Law.

I.1.2.3.4. Tax rates

Taxable profits obtained by Mexican companies are subject to income tax at the corporate rate of 30 per cent. That being said, royalty payments are no exception thereto and as such they must be accrued and income tax paid thereupon at the corporate tax rate.

Foreign tax residents with a permanent establishment status would be taxed alike at the corporate tax rate of 30 per cent regarding accruable interest payments (on the taxable basis).

Concerning foreign tax residents that receive royalty payments, the applicable withholding tax rate (on the gross amount of the consideration, without the possibility of claiming any deduction) could be of 5, 25 or 35 per cent (whilst the withholding rate applicable to technical assistance fees is of 25 per cent).

Notwithstanding the foregoing, foreign tax residents whose income is deemed as subject to a preferential tax regime pursuant to the Income Tax Law, could be subject to a 40 per cent withholding tax on royalty payments they receive (or technical assistance fees), without the possibility of claiming any deduction to reduce the taxable basis. Income tax due in such cases would be paid via withholding when the entity making the corresponding payment is a Mexican resident or a foreign tax resident with a permanent establishment within the country.

Nonetheless, pursuant to most of the double taxation agreements concluded by Mexico, whereas withholding tax on royalty payments could be capped at 10 per cent of the gross amount of the relevant consideration (royalty payment), technical assistance fees could in some cases fall under article 7 (Business Profits) and as such, could be exempted from income taxation in Mexico.

I.1.3. Special Features of the CIT system

As explained further in section 1.6 hereof, the Mexican corporate income tax system can be characterised as profoundly influenced by recent developments at an international level, such as OECD guidelines, multilateral instruments and normative projects.

In line with the above, provisions typically reserved for such international legal systems have been gradually incorporated to Mexican tax laws. For instance, under Mexican law, taxpayers conducting activities abroad could be subject to certain filing obligations derived from the OECD Common Reporting Standard (CRS).

I.1.3.1. Existence of Group Regime

As of January 2014, the consolidation tax regime was repealed from the Income Tax Law. However, an optional group regime was added in its place, named integrating regime.

In terms of the optional regime for groups of companies, two types of entities are relevant: the integrating company (*Integradora*) and the integrated companies (*Integradas*). Pursuant to the newly added regime, taxpayers may be entitled to defer, for up to three fiscal years, part of the income tax payable by both the integrating or parent company and the integrated companies taking into account losses of the parent company (several rules and requirements may apply).

For an entity to obtain the authorisation to operate under the optional regime for groups of companies, certain requirements must be met, as follows:

1. It must be a Mexican resident company.
2. Directly or indirectly hold more than 80% of the shares with voting rights of the companies that will be integrated.
3. Obtain the written consent of the legal representative of each of the companies that will be integrated.
4. File before the tax authorities a request to operate under the optional regime for groups of companies (accompanying thereto, supporting information and documentation such as the companies' shareholders and their participation therein).

It should be noted that several restrictions apply both to the integrating company and to the integrated companies. For instance, entities that form part of the financial system, foreign residents, or legal entities with non-profit purposes may not be subject to this tax regime.

I.1.3.2. Treatment of Losses

Tax losses (NOL's) will exist when the amount of authorised deductions exceeds the amount of taxable income. Tax losses may be used to reduce the taxable profit for the following ten (10) fiscal periods. In the event that the taxpayer fails to carry forward its tax loss from previous years, even though the taxpayer could have done so, the taxpayer would then forfeit the right to do so in subsequent years, for up to the amount that could have been deducted.

NOL's are also subject to inflation adjustment from the date in which they were originally incurred until the date they are used to amortise taxable income.

As a general rule, the right to amortise NOL's corresponds exclusively to the taxpayer that incurred in such losses, and may not be transferred, even as a consequence of a merger.

I.1.3.3. Tax Holidays

Tax holidays under the Income Tax Law mainly consist of specific incentives or tax regimes for various purposes, most of which are contained in Title VII of the Income Tax Law (*De los estímulos fiscales*).

As mentioned before, the tax incentives contained therein serve different purposes such as allowing specific deductions for employers that hire disables or elderly people (a tax credit for an amount equal to the 100 per cent of income tax withheld and paid by such employees) or granting tax credits for the distribution and production of cinematographic projects, for the investment in cultural projects (theatrical productions, visual arts, amongst others).

From a business perspective, other tax incentives in the form of specific tax regimes have been included in the Income Tax Law. For instance, tax deferrals concerning Mexican trusts incorporated for purposes of acquiring, developing and leasing real estate located within Mexican territory (trusts known as *FIBRAS* that can either be public or private entities, and that resemble in certain aspects to the US REITS), or more beneficial tax regimes for parties that invest in Mexican trusts incorporated to promote risk capital investments in Mexico (*FICAPS*).

Lastly, the possibility of incorporating a sole-member business corporation was recently included to the Business Corporations Act. Accordingly, a specific tax regime was tailored for these simplified business corporations.

I.2. Corporate Income Tax on International Level

Hereunder you will find a comprehensive analysis with respect to the tax consequences that could be triggered from Mexico's standpoint both by inbound and outbound transactions involving the active and passive income items studied in section 1.1. of this chapter.

I.2.1. Inbound Transactions

As per mentioned in section I.1 of this chapter, foreign tax residents could be liable for income tax in Mexico either on all income attributable to a permanent establishment of theirs located within national territory, or on income sourced therein.

In this regard, foreign tax residents planning on doing business in Mexico should keep in mind that they could acquire a permanent establishment status if any of the following conditions arises:

a. If business activities are conducted or independent personal services are rendered in Mexico. Accordingly, any branch, agency, office, manufacturing facility, workshop, mine, or any other place for the extraction, exploration or exploitation of natural resources located within Mexican territory could be deemed to constitute a permanent establishment.

b. A foreign resident could also acquire a permanent establishment status if it were to act by means of a dependent agent; and

c. A foreign resident could be deemed to have a permanent establishment in Mexico if it were to act therein by conduct of an independent agent acting beyond its ordinary course of business.

In cases were the foreign resident conducting its business were to acquire a permanent establishment status, any and all income attributable thereto would be subject to taxation in Mexico.

It should be noted that double taxation agreements concluded by Mexico would seldom be considered to provide relief regarding the avoidance of the permanent establishment status, since the criteria contained therein for purposes of identifying a permanent establishment are close to identical to those set forth in the Income Tax Law.

What is more, backed by recent developments in the international arena (i.e. BEPS Action 7), tax authorities are ever more likely to identify artificial schemes for the avoidance of the permanent establishment status, such as *commissionnaire* arrangements.

In view of the foregoing, any of such active (business profits) or passive (dividends, interests and royalties) income items mentioned in section I.1., could trigger income tax in Mexico in so far as they are attributable to a foreign resident's permanent establishment located within Mexican territory.

Moreover, foreign tax residents with a permanent establishment within Mexican territory that receive income deemed as subject to a preferential tax regime (as per the Income Tax Law) could be required to pay income tax in terms of Chapter I of Title VI of the Income Tax Law, that is, the applicable provisions for preferential tax regimes.

Income items could be considered to be subject to a preferential tax regime if: (i) they are not taxed in the foreign residents' jurisdictions; (ii) the applicable tax rate in the foreign residents' jurisdictions is lower than 75 per cent of the income tax that would have been paid in Mexico; (iii) such income items are received by conduct of foreign tax transparent legal entities or vehicles; or (iv) the relevant income items derive from a *listed jurisdiction* presumed to have a preferential tax regime pursuant to the Income Tax Law.

In general terms, the foreign resident with a permanent establishment status in Mexico that receives income deemed as subject to a preferential tax regime would be required to accrue the relevant income items as of the moment they are received by the foreign entity or vehicle (instead of having to accrue such income when attributed to the permanent establishment), that is, even without said income being distributed to the permanent establishment. Furthermore, income tax would be levied at the corporate tax rate of 30 per cent.

Regardless of the foregoing, income tax could also be triggered at the level of foreign residents whenever they are deemed to receive Mexican sourced income items. Generally speaking, income tax due by foreign residents would be paid via withholding in cases were the corresponding payment (from which taxable income derives) is made by a Mexican resident or a foreign resident with a permanent establishment located within Mexican territory. Moreover, the applicable withholding tax rate could vary depending on the relevant income item received by the foreign resident.

Irrespective of the general tax treatment to which a foreign tax resident could be subject to, in cases where Mexican-sourced income received by a foreign tax resident is deemed to be subject to a preferential tax regime in its jurisdiction (in terms of the Income Tax Law), a withholding tax at a rate of 40 per cent could result applicable (except for dividend and certain interest payments, in which case the 40 per cent tax rate would not be applicable in so far as the corresponding requirements under the general tax treatment are met).

As a general rule, income items received by a foreign tax resident could be considered as subject to a preferential tax regime whenever they are not subject to taxation in the foreign resident's jurisdiction or the applicable tax is lower than the equivalent of 75 per cent of income tax that would have been triggered in Mexico for such an operation. In addition, income could also be considered as subject to a preferential tax regime if it is received by conduct of a tax transparent legal vehicle or entity or in cases where the Mexican-sourced income is received by a tax resident of a *listed jurisdictions* in terms of the Income Tax Law.

Notwithstanding the foregoing, relief in the form of reduced withholding tax rates or even tax exemptions could be provided by means of the double taxation agreements concluded by Mexico.

Furthermore, depending on the applicable double taxation agreement, foreign residents taxed on Mexican-sourced income could be entitled to credit or deduct income tax paid in Mexico, at the level of the jurisdiction in which they are tax residents.

I.2.2. Outbound Transactions

Since Mexican resident companies are liable for income tax in Mexico on a worldwide basis, that is, on any and all income they receive irrespective from where its sourced, any income item received from abroad could be deemed as an accruable income (for purposes of determining the taxable basis for the relevant tax year and thus, income tax due). Consequently, Mexican entities obtaining income sourced in other jurisdictions would be subject to taxation in Mexico even if the corresponding income items were taxed (or not) in the jurisdictions from which they derive.

Nevertheless, either the Income Tax Law and/or the applicable double taxation agreement could allow Mexican taxpayers to mitigate or in some cases avoid the effects of double taxation (i.e. possibility of crediting income tax paid abroad).

However, it should be noted that Mexican residents could be subject to a special tax regime concerning income they receive that is deemed as subject to a preferential tax regime.

For such purposes, income items could be considered as subject to a preferential regime if they are not taxed in the foreign jurisdiction from which the applicable tax rate is lower than the equivalent of 75 per cent of the income tax that would have been paid in Mexico, in cases where they are received by conduct of fiscally transparent legal entities or vehicles or derived from a *listed jurisdiction* presumed to have a preferential tax regime, pursuant to the Income Tax Law.

Mexican tax residents would be liable for income tax due on income items subject to a preferential tax regime as of the moment in which the foreign legal entity or vehicle in which they participate receives them (such income items would be deemed as accruable income). Income tax due thereupon would be levied at the corporate tax rate of 30 per cent.

I.3. Anti-Avoidance Legislation

Concerning anti-avoidance provisions, the following rules should be kept in mind:

1. CFC rules: Mexican residents could be forced to accrue in advance profits considered to be subject to a preferential tax regime abroad, or perceived by means of a fiscally transparent legal entity or vehicle that controls or is controlled by the local taxpayer.

   Pursuant to applicable laws, profits could be considered as subject to preferential tax regimes abroad in cases where they are not taxed in the jurisdiction of origin or regardless of being taxed, it is done so at a rate lower than 75 per cent of the income tax that would have been caused in Mexico for the corresponding transaction.

2. Thin capitalisation rules: Concerning the debt contracted by a local entity and a related party located abroad, the deduction of interest payments arising

therefrom could be challenged in cases where the totality of the debt's value exceeds by threefold of the debtor's net worth. In certain cases, particularly concerning entities involved in the financial system and in the country's strategic sectors, higher debt-to-net equity ratios could be allowed given the nature and scale of the operations.

3. Back-to-back loans: Interest payments deriving from loans contracted between related parties could be challenged and re-characterised by Mexican tax authorities as a distribution of profits or dividends, thus, limiting the deduction thereof.

4. Transfer-pricing rules: In general terms, transactions between related parties are required to comply with the arm's-length principle, therefore, it should be noted that tax authorities are entitled to exercise auditing powers in order to determine whether transfer-pricing rules have been abided by in the performance of certain transactions.

   Moreover, taxpayers could be required to file transfer-pricing studies, accounting and tax documentation, as well as annual informative returns.

5. Pro rata expenses: Generally speaking, the deduction of expenses incurred abroad on a pro rata basis with foreign entities that are not subject to taxation in Mexico could be forbidden, unless certain specific requirements are met.

6. Restrictions on the deduction of interest, royalty and technical assistance payments: When interest, royalty and technical assistance payments are made by a local entity to a foreign entity that controls or is controlled by the first (in cases where the foreign entity is considered fiscally transparent, that the payment in question is deemed as non-existent for tax purposes pursuant to laws of the foreign entity's jurisdiction, or that the profits deriving therefrom are not considered as taxable in terms of the applicable foreign laws) the

deduction thereof could be forbidden.

For purposes of the foregoing, control means that one entity has effective control over the other or its administration to the extent of being able to decide (directly or indirectly) when to distribute profits or dividends.

7. Additionally, it should be noted that certain formal requirements under Mexican law ought to by abided by in order for treaty benefits to be eligible. In this regard, Mexican tax authorities could request a sworn affidavit stating the existence of double taxation and identifying the statutes or provisions under foreign law in terms of which said double taxation exists.

I.3.1. Abuse of Law

All activities conducted by taxpayers in Mexico ought to be duly recorded in compliance with the requirements set forth in corporate and tax laws. Additionally, taxpayers must be able to evidence that their transactions were indeed performed (business rationale).

In this regard, article 69-B of the Federal Tax Code sets forth the procedure that ought to be conducted by tax authorities in order to characterise as inexistent or sham transactions the activities performed by taxpayers.

In general terms, when tax authorities suspect that certain transaction did not take place or that it was simulated in order to obtain a tax benefit, they must serve notice to the corresponding taxpayer of such circumstance and are required to have published in the official gazette a list of taxpayers whose activities are deemed as inexistent or sham transactions.

The corresponding taxpayers (as well as the third parties that allegedly entered into the relevant transactions with them) are required to produce evidence with respect to such transactions. However, if they fail to evidence that the transactions were indeed performed, tax authorities would be entitled to publish a definitive list of taxpayers whose activities are deemed as inexistent (or sham transactions). What is more, tax benefits/consequences in relation to the invoices issued as a result of such transactions would be annulled by tax authorities. Furthermore, taxpayers listed therein could be subject to criminal charges.

I.3.2. Thin Capitalization Rules

Under Mexican laws, interest payments are one of the most strictly regulated deductions. In this sense, tax authorities have established stringent requirements and rules, such as thin capitalisation rules, that ought to be complied with in order for those payments to be deductible.

Pursuant to the thin capitalisation rules set forth in Mexican laws, Mexican resident entities could be entitled to deduct interest payments resulting from debt contracted with a related party abroad, as long as the relevant entity's total amount of debt does not exceed by threefold its equity, that is, the allowed debt-to-equity ratio under Mexican law is 3:1.

To calculate the amount of debt exceeding the allowed debt-to-equity ratio indicated above, the sum of the shareholders´ equity at the beginning and at the end of the tax year shall be divided by two. The quotient thereof shall be then multiplied by three, and the result shall be finally subtracted from the annual average balance of all the relevant taxpayer´s interest-accruing debts.

If the annual average balance of the taxpayer´s debts entered into with foreign resident related parties is lower than the excess amount of the debts referred above, no interest accrued on those debts may be deducted. If the annual average balance of the debts entered into with foreign resident related parties is greater than the aforementioned excess, interest accrued from said debts entered into with the foreign resident related parties shall not be deductible in an amount equal to the result of multiplying said interest by the factor obtained by dividing the excess by said balance.

Nonetheless, entities engaged in specific industries such as the financial system or the country's strategic sectors could be allowed to have a higher debt-to-net equity ratio.

I.3.3. CFC Legislation

Residents in Mexico or foreign residents with a permanent establishment status in Mexico are subject to taxation on income earned abroad when the corresponding income items are derived from a jurisdictions considered to have a preferential tax regime, whether these are received directly, or through legal entities in which they directly or indirectly participate (in their capital stock).

Said income, whether it be received in cash, goods, services or credit, and as long as it is not subject to taxation abroad or subject to a tax rate which is less than the equivalent of 75 per cent of the income tax that would have been levied in Mexico, could be subject to taxation in Mexico.

Income tax on income deriving from preferential regimes could be due even though said income had not actually been received by the Mexican residents (accrued in advanced). Notwithstanding the foregoing, in cases where the persons who receive said income do not have effective control of the management of the relevant entities subject to the preferential tax regimes, the corresponding tax would be payable until income is effectively received.

Income subject to this regime shall need to be determined each calendar year, and shall be accrued to the rest of income of the taxpayer. A rate of 30 per cent or 35 per cent shall be assessed on the taxable income, depending the nature of the taxpayer (entity or individual).

I.4. Tax Treaty Law

Mexico is both a Member State of the United Nations and of the OECD. In this regard, model conventions, multilateral instruments, guidelines and other normative projects issued by the aforementioned organisations have had a large impact on the design and implementation of tax laws in Mexico.

I.4.1. Adherence to UN or OECD MC

As per mentioned above, Mexico has been a member State of the United Nations since November 7, 1945. What is more, Mexico has been a non-permanent member of the security council of the United Nations in 1946, 1980 and 2002.

With respect to the OECD, Mexico deposited its instrument of ratification as a member State on May 18, 1994, and has since been an active member thereof.

I.4.2. Special Features commonly present on Tax Treaties

Tax treaties concluded by Mexico are based on the OECD Model Tax Conventions. Nonetheless, certain particularities can be adverted.

For instance, the tax treaty entered into by Mexico and the USA is the only Mexican treaty currently in force that allows foreign residents (US residents) to pay income tax in Mexico derived from the leasing of real estate located therein on a net basis as if the foreign resident had a permanent establishment status.

On a different subject, tax treaties concluded by Mexico still address the rendering of independent services based on article 14 of the OECD Model Tax Convention.

I.4.3. Treaties Currently in Force

As of July 2017, Mexico has concluded or is currently negotiating either double taxation agreements or tax information exchange agreements with the following countries or jurisdictions:

Germany	Bahrein	Korea
The Netherlands Antilles	Barbados	Costa Rica
Saudi Arabia	Belgium	Chile
Argentina	Belize	China
Aruba	Bermuda	Denmark
Australia	Brazil	Ecuador
Austria	Canada	Egypt
Bahamas	Colombia	United Arab Emirates
Slovenia	Estonia	Spain
United States of America	Philippines	Finland
France	Gibraltar	Guatemala
Greece	Hong Kong	Hungary
India	Indonesia	Iran
Ireland	Isle of Man	Cayman Islands
Cook Islands	Guernsey	Jersey
Marshall Islands	British Virgin Islands	Iceland
Israel	Italy	Jamaica
Japan	Kuwait	Lithuania
Lebanon	Lichtenstein	Latvia

Luxembourg	Malesia	Malta
Morocco	Monaco	Nicaragua
Norway	New Zealand	Oman
The Netherlands	Pakistan	Panama
Peru	Poland	Portugal
Qatar	United Kingdom	Czech Republic
Slovakia	Rumania	Russia
Samoa	Santa Lucia	Singapore
South Africa	Sweden	Switzerland
Thailand	Turks and Caicos Islands	Turkey
Ukraine	Uruguay	Vanuatu
Venezuela		

I.5. Community Law

N/A

I.5.1. Participation in a Community/Union

N/A

I.5.2. Rules regarding Corporate Income Taxation within the Community/Union

N/A

I.5.3. Jurisprudence regarding Corporate Income Taxation within the Community/Union

N/A

I.6. Influence of BEPS Action Plan on the Country

The BEPS Action Plan has had a major impact on the design and implementation of tax laws in Mexico. Furthermore, said document has made Mexican tax authorities aware of the everchanging nature of cross-border structures and transactions conducted by taxpayers.

As consequence thereof, provisions normally reserved to international instruments have gradually been incorporated to local statutes and regulations.

I.6.1. Adoption of rules in line with BEPS Reports

In line with the Common Reporting Standard and recent BEPS developments, filing obligations regarding transactions with related parties abroad have been included in the Income Tax Law.

Taxpayers could now be required to file (no later than on December 31 of the following tax year to which the filing obligation corresponds to) the following informative returns: (a) Master file, information concerning the structure and activities of multinational corporate groups; (b) Local file, describing the structure and activities conducted with related parties at a local level; and (c) country-by-country reporting, with respect to the activities, distribution of income and taxes paid in each jurisdiction.

On a different subject, it should be noted that more stringent requirements concerning the deductibility of certain income/expense items have been incorporated to Mexican laws in view of recent BEPS advances. For instance, in order for taxpayers to be able to claim treaty benefits, tax authorities could request a sworn affidavit from the foreign party stating the existence of a double taxation and identifying the statutes or provisions under foreign law in terms of which said double taxation exists.

I.6.2. Participation in Multilateral Instrument

In 2010, Mexico, as an active member of the OECD, subscribed the Convention on Mutual Administrative Assistance in Tax Matters and its Protocol. More recently, on June 7, 2017, Mexico adhered to the Multilateral Convention to Implement Tax Treaty Related Measures to Prevent Base Erosion and Profit Shifting.

I.7. Jurisprudence

Mexico's legal system can be characterised as a civil law legal system (as opposed to a common law legal system). Nevertheless, jurisprudence or precedents are deemed as sources of law.

However, it should be noted that jurisprudence derived from Mexican courts' rulings can be either binding on non-binding to other courts depending on whether certain procedural requirements are met.

I.7.1. Inbound Transactions

Since the Mexican legal system follows civil law tradition, jurisprudence at an international level is generally considered as a set of guidelines for the construction or interpretation of provisions.

I.7.2. Outbound Transactions

As mentioned above, the Mexican legal system tends to conceive jurisprudence as a set of guidelines for the construction or interpretation of provisions.

6

Peru

MR. FERNANDO NUÑEZ

I.1 Corporate Income Tax at Domestic level

I.1.1. Active Income

I.1.1.1. Business Profits

Profits obtained by legal entities resident in Peru are subject to Corporate Income Tax on a worldwide basis at a rate of 29.5%. This tax is calculated on an annual basis.

I.1.1.1.1. Taxable Event

According to the Peruvian Income Tax Law (hereinafter, the "PITL"), the following income is subject to taxation in Peru: income arising from capital, labor and the joint application of both factors; capital gains; income derived from operations with third parties; and, also presumptive income.

I.1.1.1.2. Taxable Basis

Since Peruvian legal entities are taxed on their net income, they are allowed to deduct expenses to the extent that they are necessary to produce taxable income or to maintain its source.

Some deductibility requirements and limitations may be applicable for the deduction of certain expenses, such as financial expenses (thin-capitalization rule), bad debt provisions, salaries, travel expenses, donations, among others.

For Corporate Income Tax purposes, the taxable year starts on January 1st of each year and ends on December 31st.

I.1.1.1.3. Taxpayers

The Corporate Income Tax is due by legal persons which are defined as: (i) legal entities residents in Peru (either corporations, partnerships, etc.); and (ii) branches, agencies and representative offices of non-resident entities. The definition of corporate residency is provided on the PITL, which states that the company is resident in the state in which it is incorporated. Furthermore, the PITL determines that partnerships, consortiums, joint ventures with independent accounting from its contracting parties shall be treated in the same manner as legal persons. Thus, under the Peruvian legislation unincorporated entities are also subject to Corporate Income Tax.

I.1.1.1.4. Tax rates

Effective from 1 January 2017, the Corporate Income Tax rate is 29.5% and it is applicable over the annual net income.

I.1.2. Passive Income

I.1.2.1. Dividends

Dividends distributed from Peruvian companies are not subject to Corporate Income Taxation, (full domestic participation exemption is applicable).

I.1.2.2. Interest

Interest income will be levied at the rate mentioned on section I.1.1.1.4.

I.1.1.3. Royalties

Royalties income will be levied at the rates mentioned on section I.1.1.1.4.

I.1.3. Special Features of the CIT system

I.1.3.1. Existence of Group Regime

There is no Group Regime or Tax Consolidation System.

I.1.3.2. Treatment of Losses

Resident entities must make a distinction between Peruvian-source losses and foreign-source losses.

Peruvian-source losses incurred in a fiscal year may be either (i) set off against Peruvian-source income or foreign-source income of the same year or (ii) carry forward in the subsequent years under the rules detailed below.

Losses incurred may be carried forward under the following systems:

1. Losses incurred in a year may be carried forward and set off against profits obtained in the following 4 years counted as form the following year to which the losses are reported; or
2. Losses incurred in a year may be carried forward and set off against 50% of future profits without limitation of time.

The option should be exercised when filing the Annual Corporate Income Tax Return.

There is no carry-back of losses.

Foreign-source losses may not be set off against Peruvian-source income. Foreign-source losses may only be offset against foreign-source income, i.e. all foreign-source income and losses from different activities or countries are pooled together in order to determine the foreign source net result.

I.2. Corporate Income Tax on International Level

In this section we will focus on taxation of income in inbound and outbound situations. "Inbound transactions" refers to non-residents entities in Peru with Peruvian source income. A typical inbound circumstance exists where a foreign corporation has income and/or activities in Peru.

On the other hand, the "outbound transactions" refers to resident entities in Peru with foreign source income. A typical outbound circumstance exists where a Peruvian entity has income and/or activities in other countries.

I.2.1. Inbound Transactions

As a general rule, non-resident entities in Peru are subject to Income Tax only over their Peruvian source income.

I.2.1.1 Taxation on the sale of goods

Income derived by a non-resident by the sale of goods or rights situated or economically used in Peru are subject to the income tax. The applicable rate would be 30%.

If the income is earned through a branch or other permanent establishment situated in Peru, this PE will bear the same tax burden as a tax resident, i.e. 29.5%.

I.2.1.2 Taxation of the provision of services

Income resulting from services provided within the Peruvian territory by a non-resident entities is considered to be from a Peruvian source and hence, subject to the general 30% withholding tax (hereinafter, "WHT") rate.

If the services qualify as technical assistance services or digital services, the income would be taxed in Peru, regardless the place of rendering, provided the services are economically used therein.

Technical assistance services are subject to a 15% tax rate provided some requirements are fulfilled. Digital services are subject to the general 30% tax rate.

I.2.1.3 Dividend Income

The Dividend Tax applies to profits distributed to non-residents and individuals. Hence, dividends distribution performed by Peruvian entities in favor of its non-resident shareholders would be subject to the dividend WHT.

Effective as from 1 January 2017, the dividends withholding tax rate is 5%. This rate applies to dividends related to profits generated as from such date. Profits generated up to 31 December 2014 are subject to a withholding tax rate of 4.1%, and profits generated between 1 January 2015 and 31 December 2016 are subject to a withholding tax rate at a rate of 6.8%, even if the relevant profits are distributed in 2017 and beyond.

The Income Tax Law specifies several transactions that are considered profits distributions by resident entities for purposes of the Dividends Tax. These transactions include the distribution of assets, other than shares of the distributing company, and, under certain circumstances, a capital reduction, a loan to a shareholder or the liquidation of the company.

For permanent establishments, branches, and agencies of foreign companies, a distribution of profits is deemed to occur on the deadline for filing their annual corporate income tax return (usually at the end of March or the beginning of April of the following tax year).

I.2.1.4 Interest

Interest sourced in Peru and paid to a foreign entity is subject to the 4.99% WHT rate provided the following requirements are met:

1. For loans in cash, the proceeds of the loan are brought into Peru through local banks.
2. The proceeds of the loan are used for business purposes in Peru.
3. The loan is granted by a non-related party.
4. The interest rate does not exceed Libor rate plus a spread of 7% (which includes expenses, commissions and any other amounts in addition to the interest paid).

If the conditions (a), (b) or (c) above are not satisfied, the interest is subject to the regular WHT of 30%. On the other hand, if condition (d) is not satisfied, only the excess interest over the Libor + 7% will be subject to a 30% WHT.

I.2.1.5 Royalties

Royalties paid to a foreign entity are also subject to 30% WHT.

I.2.1.6 Payments to low tax jurisdictions or fiscal privileged regimes

Expenses resulting from transactions carry out with residents in low tax jurisdictions or tax havens are not deductible for tax purposes, except for the following transactions: (i) toll payment for the right to use the Panama

Channel; (ii) expenses related to loan operations, (iii) insurance or reinsurance payments, (iv) leasing of ships or aircraft and freight services to and from Peru.

The Peruvian Tax Law have included several jurisdictions in a low-tax jurisdictions "black list".

In addition to the jurisdictions included in the "black list", other jurisdictions may be considered low-tax jurisdictions if its effective corporate Income Tax rate is 14.5% or lower and to the extent the one of the following additional conditions is met:

- The jurisdiction does not provide information regarding the taxation of resident companies.
- A tax benefit regime applies exclusively to non-resident entities which carried out activities in that jurisdiction.
- Only offshore activities are accepted as a condition to apply a tax benefit regime.
- The jurisdiction promotes itself as a jurisdiction that can assist companies to reduce the tax liabilities in its countries of origin.

I.2.2. Outbound Transactions

Entities resident in Peru are subject to the Corporate Income Tax on a worldwide basis. Thus both Peruvian source income and foreign income of any type are subject to the 29.5% Corporate Income Tax rate.

I.2.2.1 Taxation on the sale of goods

See answer I.2.1.1.

I.2.2.1 Taxation of the provision of services

See answer I.2.1.1.

I.2.2.3 Dividend Income

See answer I.2.1.1.

I.2.2.4 Interest

See answer I.2.1.1.

I.2.2.5 Royalties

See answer I.2.1.1.

I.3. Anti-Avoidance Legislation

I.3.1. General Anti-Avoidance rule

Pursuant to Peruvian General Anti-Avoidance Rule, the Peruvian Tax Authority is legally entitled to challenge so-called sham transactions and tax avoidance cases.

Sham transactions consist in *"presenting some fact or event that is apparent (illusory) and not real or disguising any fact or act and exposing other instead"*. To this respect, doctrine distinguishes between "absolute sham", in which there is no real legal business; and, "relative sham" in which there is indeed a real legal business but it differs from the business that is exposed to third parties.

Sham transactions are challenged by means of Rule XVI of the Preliminary Tittle of the Peruvian Tax Code (hereinafter, "Rule XVI"), according to the amendments introduced by the Legislative Decree No. 1121 (in force since July 19th, 2012). SUNAT was also entitled to challenge the sham transactions under the previous Rule VIII of the Peruvian Tax Code that was in force until it was amended by Rule XVI.

On the other hand, tax fraud (tax avoidance) is defined as a legal structure carried out on the framework of a civil rule, corporate rule, commercial rule or any combination of the above (this is called the "coverage rule"), which allows the parties to achieve the desired commercial objective, without fitting in the taxable event of a tax rule.

As of July 19th, 2012, under Rule XVI, SUNAT is also entitled to challenge transactions that configure a tax fraud. Rule XVI establishes that in order to determine the true nature of a taxable event, SUNAT will take into account the acts, situations and economic relations that the taxpayers effectively perform or pursue.

For this purpose, tax fraud will be configured when the realization of the taxable event is totally or partially avoided, when the tax base or tax debt is reduced, or credits or tax losses are obtained by carrying out acts where the following circumstances, which must be proved by SUNAT, occur concurrently:

1. The acts, individually or jointly carried out by the parties are artificial or improper to achieve the obtained result.
2. The acts celebrated by the parties, because of their use, generate legal or economic effects, different from tax saving or tax advantages; effects that could be equal or similar to those obtained with the usual or proper acts.

If both conditions are verified, SUNAT shall be allowed to re-qualify the adopted business form and to apply the tax consequences that would have corresponded to usual or proper acts, as appropriate.

However, it is worth noting that the application of Rule XVI to tax fraud cases is suspended until the Government sets out the parameters of form and base that are within the scope of the Rule XVI.

There is uncertainty on whether these parameters will be issued soon or issued at all.

I.3.2. Thin Capitalization Rules

Interest paid by resident entities to related parties (either resident or not) will not be deductible in the portion that exceeds the result of applying a coefficient (debt/equity ratio) equivalent to three times the taxpayer's net equity at the end of the preceding year (3:1). In the case of newly incorporated entities, the coefficient would be equivalent to 3 times their net equity at the time of their incorporation.

Therefore, interest paid or payable to related parties that does not exceed in 3 times the taxpayer's net equity at the end of the preceding year -or at the time of its incorporation- would be deductible for the entity for Peruvian Income Tax purposes. However, if at any moment of the fiscal year such interest exceeds the limit; it would only be proportionally deductible.

I.3.3. CFC Legislation

Peru's "Controlled Foreign Company Rules" (CFC Rules) have been in force since January 1, 2013. This new regime is applicable to any Peruvian resident, who controls a non-resident entity that, according to the law, qualifies as a Controlled Foreign Company (CFC) regarding their passive income. Thus, CFC Rules shall be applicable to passive income received (not necessarily distributed) by a company directly or indirectly controlled by a Peruvian resident.

A non-resident company shall be deemed controlled by a Peruvian resident when, at the end of the fiscal year (December 31), directly or indirectly (solely or together with any related party) holds more than 50% of the equity, benefits or voting rights of the non-resident entity (hereinafter, 50%Test).

A controlled foreign company is defined as any entity of any nature, non-resident in the country, which meets the following requirements:

1. It has a legal personality independent from its partners, associates, members or owners. Companies, investment funds, trusts, partnerships, associations and foundations are considered as legal separate entities for purposes of the CFC Rules;
2. It is incorporated, established or considered as resident in countries or territories with no or low taxation, or in countries or territories where the passive income is not subject to Income Tax, or where the applicable tax rate on similar income is equal or less than 75% of the tax rate which would apply in Peru; and,
3. It is owned by a Peruvian resident taxpayer (individual or entity).

I.4. Tax Treaty Law

I.4.1. Adherence to UN or OECD MC

Almost all the Treaties signed by Peru follows the OECD Model Tax Convention and also includes some features from the UN Model Tax Convention.

By way of exception, the Andean Treaty (Decision 578) follows mostly exclusive taxation at the country of source.

I.4.2. Special Features commonly present on Tax Treaties

Some of the Peru Tax Treaties includes some features of the UN Model Convention such as a broad definition of PE (including the services PE), taxation at source in the case of royalties and interest, a broad definition of royalties, among others.

I.4.3. Treaties Currently in Force

Peru has signed treaties with Chile, Canada, Brazil, Switzerland, South Korea, Mexico and Portugal.

In addition, Peru has signed the Andean Pact (Decision 578) with Colombia, Ecuador and Bolivia.

I.5. Community Law

I.5.1. Participation in a Community/Union

Peru is part of the Andean Community. The Andean Community is a customs union comprising the South American countries of Bolivia, Colombia, Ecuador, and Peru

I.5.2. Rules regarding Corporate Income Taxation within the Community/Union

Not applicable.

I.5.3. Jurisprudence regarding Corporate Income Taxation within the Community/Union

Not applicable

I.6. Influence of BEPS Action Plan on the Country

I.6.1. Adoption of rules in line with BEPS Reports

Within the last tax reform enacted in the year 2016, Peru has adopted Action 13 regarding Transfer Pricing Documentation and CbC Reporting.

The new standards will enter into force on year 2017 provided the Regulations are enacted. Up to date, Regulations about this matter are still pending.

I.6.2. Participation in Multilateral Instrument

Peru has not yet signed the Multilateral Instrument.

However, the Government has unofficially announced its intention to sign it shortly.

I.7. Jurisprudence

I.7.1. Inbound Transactions

Not applicable.

I.7.2. Outbound Transactions

Not applicable.

7

Venezuela

MR. WINSTON PEREZ

I.1 Corporate Income Tax at Domestic level

The Venezuelan Constitution provides for a tax system based on a fair distribution of tax, levied according to the economic capacity of the taxpayer, the principle of progressive rates, the protection of the national economy, and the upgrade of the living standard of Venezuelan citizens.

I.1.1. Active Income

I.1.1.1. Business Profits

Availability of Income

In general terms, most items will be taxed on an accrual basis. However, the Venezuelan Income Tax Law (from herein VITL) provides three exceptions to this general rule: (a) in case of credit assignments and discount operations whose product recovers in various annuities, income is considered available for the assignee in proportion to the corresponding benefit; (b) income from loans granted by banks, insurance companies and other credit institutions and from lease and sublease of movable and immovable property is considered available when accrued in a specific fiscal year; and (c) income from work under dependency relation and from gambling is considered available when paid.

Revenue

Constituted by the total amount of the sales of goods and services, leasing and any other regular or sporadic activities such as those arising from work performed under an employment relationship or from the practice of non-mercantile professions, as well as those derived from royalties or similar shares, except where otherwise established by the Law.

Gross Profits

Determined by deducting the cost of the products transferred and services rendered in the country from the revenue, unless the nature of the activity thereof requires the application of different procedures.

Gross profits derived from foreign source will be determined by subtracting from their revenues the foreign costs imputable to same. Costs and common deductions applicable to revenues of territorial or extraterritorial source will be proportionally distributed to the respective revenues.

The law stipulates that acquisition costs of those goods which are to be resold or transformed in the country, customary commissions charged for procedures associated with the acquisition of goods, as well as transport and insurance are deemed incurred in the country. These costs should be invoiced at values which may not exceed the fair market value.

I.1.1.1.1. Taxable Event

For Venezuelan Corporate Income Tax purposes the taxable event would be earnings obtained in or outside the country at the end of the fiscal year. Thus, tax is levy on a current year basis. The tax year adopted is generally that specified in a company's statutory documents with the standard year being a calendar year. However, it should be noted that other periods are also allowed. The tax is payable when filing the final corporate tax return, required within three months of the end of the fiscal year.

I.1.1.1.2. Taxable Basis

The tax is levy on net earnings; which means, equity increases resulting after subtracting costs and deductions allowed by the Law from gross income, as the case may be, from the aggregate net earnings and then, the corresponding progressive tariff is applied. Taxpayers not designated as "Special" by the Venezuelan National Tax Agency" (SENIAT) or that do not engage in baking, financial, insurance or reinsurance activities must add or subtract the result from inflation adjustment before applying the tariff.

Deductions

For the determination of net global earnings, the VITL establishes certain expenses and conditions that must be complied with for deductibility purposes.

Net income is determined by subtracting from the gross profits certain deductions that must correspond to disbursements not imputable to the cost, and which must be customary, incurred in the country and necessary for the production of income.

Customary and necessary expenses incurred in Venezuela associated with the export of goods produced in the country or services rendered abroad are also deductible.

Normal and necessary expenses incurred abroad or incurred in Venezuela relating to revenues from abroad will be distributed in a manner proportional to the respective revenues.

Among the most important expenses are the following:

a. Salaries of personnel: Salaries paid to both domestic and foreign employees are deductible. Deductions for salaries paid to directors, managers and administrators are limited to a maximum 15% of gross income. Likewise, the Tax Administration is entitled to reject payments associated with salaries and other concepts related to any excess in the percentage stipulated in the Venezuelan Labor Law (20%), for payroll of expatriate personnel.

b. Paid Taxes: The VITL allows for deduction of taxes which have been effectively paid in connection with the production of income, such as municipal business tax, tax on urban property, social contributions, etc.

c. Amortization and depreciation: Expenses arising from depreciation of fixed assets and amortization of the cost of other elements invested in the production of income are deductible, provided that such goods are located in the country. Only real properties invested as fixed assets and those leased to employees may be deducted. Generally, the straight-line and the unit-of-production depreciation methods are acceptable for tax purposes. SENIAT may authorize any generally accepted method of depreciation; however, a change in method requires prior authorization. No official depreciation tables have been established.

d. Bad Debts: Deduction of losses from bad accounts requires the fulfillment of the following conditions: (i) That the debt relates to operations inherent to the business; (ii) That the amount has been taken into account when calculating the gross taxable income declared, except in the case of losses affecting capitals made available by financial institutions, or in the case of losses associated with loans granted by companies to their employees (iii) The debtor is declared insolvent or the amount indebted does not justify collection expenses.

e. Loses associated with goods used in the production of income: Losses from fixed assets used in the production of income which have not been compensated by insurance may be deducted, provided that said losses have not been imputed to the cost.

f. Interests: Interest expenses incurred for the production of income are deductible whether the interest is paid abroad or to a local company. Thin capitalization rules apply when interest is paid to a related party and limitations on the amount deductible will be applicable.

g. Charitable contributions: Deductions for allowable charitable contributions are limited to 10% of taxable income (before deducting contributions) when taxable income does not exceed 10.000 Tax Units[1]. When taxable income exceeds 10.000 Tax Units, charitable contributions are limited to 8% of taxable income.

h. Royalties: Payment of royalties to a parent company or affiliates abroad is permitted without authorization. The legal definition of royalty includes the assignment of the use of trademarks, logos, and brand names subject to patenting.

i. Technical assistance: Technical assistance is legally understood as the supply of instructions, printed information, recordings, films and other similar technical information, for the purpose of producing a sales product or specific service. This includes the transfer of know-how, engineering services, research and

---

[1] Tax Unit was introduced in 1994 as an element that reduces the negative effects created by inflation on the determination of tax rates and penalties. The value of the Tax Unit is adjusted annually according to the variation of the consumer price index from the previous year. For 2016 1 Tax Unit equals VEF 177.

development projects, advising and consulting, and the supply of procedures, formulas of production, data, information, technical specifications, diagrams, plans, technical manuals, basic and specific engineering supplies. Training and educational expenses are excluded from the definition of technical assistance. Expenses for technical assistance paid to foreign companies will be non-deductible if these services could have been rendered within Venezuela. In this regard, taxpayers must show to the Tax Administration documents evidencing the arrangements done in order to obtain the aforementioned services within the country. Also, all payments for services that are not necessary for the production process or for the execution of the service are excluded from this definition.

j. Technological services: The VITL defines fees for technological services to be amounts paid for the use of or enjoyment of industrial patents and trademarks or rights of exploration of or exploitation of natural resources, regardless of how they are describe in the contract. As in the case for technical assistance, expenses for technological services paid to foreign companies will be non-deductible if these services could have been rendered within Venezuela. Taxpayers must show to the Tax Administration documents evidencing the arrangements done in order to obtain the aforementioned services within the country

k. Intercompany charges: Intercompany transactions such as the payment of professional services and commissions, and general and administrative expenses to foreign affiliated companies must be adequately documented in order to be deductible (debit notes are not sufficient).

I.1.1.1.3. Taxpayers

The Venezuelan Income Tax law (VITL)[2] adopts the taxation regime based on worldwide income. According to this regime, resident individuals or companies domiciled in Venezuela will pay taxes for the entirety of their annual net and available earnings, obtained in or outside the country. Individuals or companies domiciled abroad with a permanent establishment or fixed base in Venezuela will be subject to tax on the worldwide income attributable to the permanent establishment or fixed place of business. Non-resident individuals or non-domiciled companies will be subject to this tax only when the source or cause of earnings lies within the country, even if they do not have permanent establishment or fixed base in Venezuela.

I.1.1.1.4. Tax rates

The VITL provides three (3) types of tariff classification of progressive tax rates, applicable according to the kind of taxpayer and the activity performed:

a. Tariff N° 1, applicable to individuals and taxpayers assimilated under this category, which establishes rates ranging from six percent (6%) to a maximum of thirty four percent (34%);

b. Tariff N° 2, applicable to stock companies and taxpayers assimilated under this category who carry out activities other than hydrocarbon or related activities, with establishes rates ranging from fifteen percent (15%) to a maximum of thirty four percent (34%). Companies that engage in banking, financial, insurance or reinsurance activities will be taxed with a proportional tax of forty percent (40%) ; and

---

2 Published in Venezuelan Official Gazette N° 6.210 dated December 30, 2015.

c. Tariff 3, applicable to applicable to royalties obtained by mining and oil companies, which establishes rates of sixty percent (60%) and fifty percent (50%), for enrichments derived from mining royalties, and enrichments obtained by oil companies, respectively.

Capital Gains

Capital gains are taxable as ordinary income, and capital losses are deductible from ordinary income. Capital losses resulting from the sale of stock, capital reduction or liquidation of a company are only deductible if they meet one of the following conditions:

a. The cost of the capital stock was not in excess of the price quoted on a stock exchange or an amount with a reasonable relationship to the book value of the capital stock.
b. The holding period of the investment was for at least two years immediately preceding the date of the sale.
c. The stockholder proves that the company selling the shares carried on economic activities for at least two years preceding the date of the sale.

I.1.2. Passive Income

I.1.2.1. Dividends

The VITL provides for a proportional tax of 34% levied on dividends arising from the payer's Net Income that exceed the Net Fiscal Taxed Income. Therefore, it only applies to the portion not previously taxed at the corporate level. Net Income is understood to be the approved income in a Shareholders' Meeting according to the Venezuelan GAAP and serves as the base for dividend distribution. As in the case of Net Fiscal Taxed Income, the Net Income is subject to the respective tax rate. When the dividends are paid by companies engaged in the exploitation of hydrocarbons the tax rate will be 50% and if the dividends are generated by companies dedicated to the exploitation of mines, the tax rate will be 60%.

Dividends received from foreign companies shall be subject to a proportional tax of 34%, having the beneficiary of the dividend the possibility of attributing the foreign tax paid for this concept.

Share dividends shall be subject to a prepaid tax of 1% over the value of the declared dividend. Individuals or companies receiving share dividends must declare and pay the total amount of the proportional tax on dividends, upon the sale of the referred to stock.

I.1.2.2. Interest

Unless the debtor can prove otherwise, any sum paid by a debtor in excess of the principal is deemed to be interest. As a general rule, interest is sourced in Venezuela if it is derived from activities carried out in Venezuela or from property located in Venezuela. Specifically, interest is deemed to be derived from activities carried out in Venezuela if the loan principal is used or enjoyed in the country. Interest received by non-resident corporations is therefore subject to Venezuelan income tax if the loan is granted or invested in Venezuela.

Interest paid on loans granted by non-resident financial institutions is subject to a final withholding tax (WHT) at source at a rate of 4.95% on gross income. Interest paid to other non-resident legal entities is subject to tax at a rate of 34% applied to 95% of the gross income.

I.1.1.3. Royalties

Royalties derived by Venezuelan residents is consider ordinary income for income tax purposes.

Royalties received by non-residents are subject to income tax on 90% of gross receipts in the case of royalties and similar payments, other than those derived from mining activities, resulting in an effective WHT rate of 30.6%.

I.1.3. Special Features of the CIT system

Deemed Income

The concept of deemed income is applied to those cases where the Tax Authorities encounter difficulties in estimating the income obtained by the taxpayer, when such taxpayer is domiciled or residing abroad and does not have a permanent establishment in the country.

The VITL provides the application of a special tax regime called "Deemed Income", which is determined based on gross income obtained by the taxpayer from abroad for activities carried out in the country and applying a percentage which the Law assumes that has been earned on such gross income.

Among other presumptive revenues are:

a. Transport services from abroad. Their net income is equivalent to ten percent (10%) of their gross profit. The latter shall be represented by fifty percent (50%) of the amount of the freights and ticket fares between Venezuela and abroad and vice versa, and by the entire income arising from freights in Venezuela.

b. Net earnings obtained by taxpayers who ship merchandise on consignment from abroad to Venezuela, will be equivalent to twenty five percent (25%) of their gross profit.

c. Net income associated with fees paid to nonresidents in Venezuela or non-domiciled companies is deemed to be ninety percent (90%) of their gross profit.

d. Net income derived from technical assistance or technological services will be constituted by amounts representing thirty percent (30%) of the gross profit obtained by reason of technical assistance, and fifty percent (50%) of gross profit obtained in compensation for technological services.

e. Net income derived from royalties and other similar participations is deemed ninety percent (90%) of the gross profit.

Tax Adjustment for Inflation

The Venezuelan Tax Reform promulgated and published in the Official Gazette N° 4,300 of August 13, 1991 introduced inflation adjustment mechanisms for tax purposes on January 1, 1993. The system adopted in 1991 is mainly in force at this date. There is no obligation to record these adjustments in the taxpayer's statutory accounting books. Currently, companies engages in banking, financial, insurance and reinsurance activities and companies designated as "Special Taxpayers" by SENIAT are excluded from the adjustment for inflation system. The main provisions concerning adjustment for inflation are summarized as follows.

The system provides two types of adjustments:

• An initial adjustment of depreciable fixed assets that will require a registry tax of 3% of said adjustment.
• An annual adjustment that is to be applied each year when determining the taxpayer's net taxable income.

Both adjustments are mandatory for taxpayers carrying out commercial, industrial, financial, and insurance operations, as well as exploitation of mines and hydrocarbons. Both adjustments are optional for taxpayers performing non- commercial activities.

Initial Adjustment

This adjustment has to be made at the closing date of the tax year in which the preoperative stage ends. For this purpose, the preoperative stage ends when the first invoice is issued. The initial adjustment is applicable to all non-monetary assets and non-monetary liabilities except the assets and liabilities in foreign currency. The resulting initial adjustment will increase or decrease the tax equity to be adjusted in the annual adjustments.

The initial adjustment is calculated by applying the variation between the National Consumer Price Index (INPC) prevailing in the month in which the non-monetary assets or liabilities were acquired and the month in which the first operating fiscal period ends. Assets acquired prior to 1950 are deemed to have been acquired in January 1950.

A registry tax of three percent (3%) is applied exclusively to the initial revaluation adjustment of depreciable fixed assets. For the payment of such tax, taxpayers must be registered in the Revalued Asset Registry established by the Tax Administration. The resulting tax can be paid in three (3) consecutive annual installments beginning at the date of registration.

Depreciation or amortization on the revaluation adjustment is allowed based on the original estimated useful life of the assets. When assets subject to this adjustment are transferred or sold, the non-depreciated or non-amortized amount of the revaluation will form part of the sale cost.

Annual Adjustment

This adjustment is applied to tax periods after the tax year in which the initial adjustment took place. The accounts must be adjusted by applying the adjustment factor to the items of the balance sheet at the closing dates; the resulting annual adjustment will increase or decrease taxable income.

Income Tax Withholdings

The withholding tax corresponds to the amount discounted by the payer to the beneficiary of income, equivalent to the entire or partial amount of tax due. The objective of this system is the advanced collection of tax payment as well as the control measures in regards to the income obtained by taxpayers.

The VITL has designated as withholding agent, among others, the debtors of net or gross income, salaries, wages and similar. In this regard, withholding agents are responsible before the National Treasury for any tax withheld and not paid, and are jointly liable along with the taxpayers for taxes not withheld. Further, in the event of excess or unauthorized withholdings, withholding agents are liable before taxpayers for the corresponding tax.

The law provides the obligation of payers of net or gross income to apply withholding tax to resident or nonresidents individuals or companies (domiciled or not) for services rendered by contractors and sub-contractors, leasing of goods, advertising services and professional fees, among others. Such withholding tax must be applied according to the withholding rates established in the Decree 1.808 on the Income Tax Law Partial Regulations Regarding Withholdings.

The withholding tax must be applied at the time the amount is paid or credited to account whichever occurs first. The latter corresponds to amounts recorded in the accounting of debtors, by means of nominative entries in favor of their creditors, for being credits which are legally demandable at the date of entry. This should be notified to the beneficiaries by means of credit notes, signed by the debtors, within the first five business days following the accounting record. According to our legislation, payments in kind are not subject to withholding.

Main categories of income subject to withholding taxes in Venezuela are as follows:

	Withholding percentage on the amount paid or credited into account			
	Individual		Companies	
Concept	Resident	Non-resident	Domiciled	Non-domiciled
Professional fees	3%	34%	5%	30.6% (1)
Financial commissions	3%	34%	5%	5%
Interests	3%	34%	5%	32.30% (2)
Interests (Foreign financial institutions)				4.95%
Contractors and Sub-contractors for rendering services	1%	34%	2%	34%
Lease of real estate	3%	34%	5%	34%
Lease of chattel	3%	34%	5%	5%
Sale of trust fund	3%	34%	5%	5%
Sale of stock exchange	1%	1%	1%	1%
Sale of unlisted stock	3%	34%	5%	5%
Royalties and similar participation		30.6% (3)		30.6% (3)

Technical assistance		10.2% (4)		10.2% (4)
Technology services		17% (5)		17% (5)
Freights in Venezuela	1%		3%	
Freights to International transportation companies				1.7% (6)

1) Withholding effective rate: maximum tranche (34%) of the progressive rate for legal entities (rate N°2) over an alleged tax basis of 90%.

2) Withholding effective rate: maximum tranche (34%) of Rate N°2 over an alleged tax basis of 95%. (3) Withholding effective rate: maximum tranche (34%) of Rate N°2 over an alleged tax basis of 90%.

3) Withholding effective rate: maximum tranche (34%) of Rate N°2 over an alleged tax basis of 30%.

4) Withholding effective rate: maximum tranche (34%) of Rate N°2 over an alleged tax basis of 50%.

5) Withholding effective rate: maximum tranche (34%) of Rate N°2 over an alleged tax basis of 5%.

Transfer Pricing

The transfer pricing regime is a mechanism of fiscal control that pursues the avoidance of artificial prices or any compensation used in the transfer of goods and services between linked parties, which may damage the fiscal income of the jurisdictions involved, cause double imposition and propitiate litigiousness between fiscal administration parties.

The Venezuelan transfer pricing rules adopt the arm's-length standard for related party transactions, adhere to the Organization for Economic Co-operation and Development (OECD) Guidelines, eliminate the safe harbor regime and impose transfer pricing documentation and filing requirements and contain APA (Administrative Provisions Act) provisions.

Related parties are defined as parties that are directly or indirectly managed, controlled or owned by the same party or group, intermediary agents and any relationship between a Venezuelan taxpayer and entities located in low-tax jurisdictions (i.e. a country included in the list of tax havens). The arm's-length standard applies to all transactions, including transfers of tangible and intangible property, services and financial arrangements.

The arm's length principle stands of transfer pricing states that the amount charged by one related party to another for a given product must be the same as if the parties were not related. This standard applies to all transactions, including transfers of tangible and intangible property, services and financial arrangements.

The transfer pricing methods specified in the Venezuelan Income Tax Law are essentially the same as those contained in the OECD Guidelines:

- Comparable uncontrolled price method.
- Resale price method.
- Cost plus method.
- Profit split method.
- Transactional net margin method.

The VITL specifically provides that the preferred method is the Comparable uncontrolled price method.

I.1.3.1. Existence of Group Regime

There is no provision for consolidated tax returns in the VITL.

I.1.3.2. Treatment of Losses

The VITL provides that net operating losses can be carryforward for three years, however the amount of losses available for carryforward may not exceed twenty five percent of the tax period's taxable income. Additionally, the VITL provides that segregated loss carryforwards (i.e., foreign operating or domestic operating) may be use only against future income of the same type (i.e., foreign operating or domestic operating). Losses derived from inflationary adjustments cannot be carryforward.

I.1.3.3. Tax Holidays

Tax holidays are not provided in the VITL.

I.2. Corporate Income Tax on International Level

I.2.1. Inbound Transactions

There is no differentiation on the tax treatment on international. Low Tax Regimes are only important for the application of the CFC rules detailed below in Chapter I.3.3. The definition of PE, Branch Income and treatment of foreign tax credits may be included in this chapter:

Permanent establishment (PE)

According to the VITL, generally, a passive party is deemed to be carrying out operations in Venezuela through a PE when:

- The passive party owns, directly or through an agent, employee, or representative in the Venezuelan territory,:
    - an office, fixed place of business, or an activity centre where its activities are totally or partially carried on

- ◦ management headquarters, branches, offices, factories, shops, facilities, warehouses, stores, construction, installations, or assembling works, when the duration thereof exceeds six months, or
- ◦ agencies or representatives authorised (according to the VITL) to contract in the name of or on behalf of the passive party.
- The passive party performs, directly or through an agent, employee, or representative in the Venezuelan territory, professional, artistic activities.
- The passive party possesses, directly or through an agent, employee, representative, or other contracted personnel in the Venezuelan territory, other work places where the operations are wholly or partially performed.

Any agent acting independently shall be excluded from this definition, except if such representative has the power to conclude contracts in the name of the principal.

Branch Income

Branches of foreign corporations are subject to the same tax rules as Venezuelan corporations. Inter-branch income and deductions must be eliminated. The positive difference between a branch's annual book and taxable income is deemed to be remitted to the branch's head office (branch profits tax). Such remittances are subject to the 34% flat dividend tax regardless of whether there is an actual payment unless the branch can provide proof of reinvestment of its profits for a five-year period. If such proof is established, no deemed remittance is assumed.

Foreign tax credit

Foreign income tax paid on taxable foreign income may be offset by the payable Venezuelan tax, up to the proportion of Venezuelan payable tax related to foreign-source income. Taxpayers must keep documentation of foreign tax. No carryforward rules are provided for in domestic regulations.

I.2.2. Outbound Transactions

There is no differentiation on the tax treatment on international. Low Tax Regimes are only important for the application of the CFC rules detailed below in Chapter I.3.3

I.3. Anti-Avoidance Legislation

The Venezuelan Master Tax Code provides that the tax authority has the power to re-characterize or denied for tax purposes the incorporation of companies, contracts and in general any legal form adopted by the taxpayer when it is determined that is was created/adopted to avoid taxes in Venezuela.

I.3.1. Abuse of Law

There are no specific abuse of law provisions established in the Venezuelan tax regulations.

I.3.2. Thin Capitalization Rules

Thin capitalization rules limit the deduction of interests from debt with related parties in excess of a 1:1 debt-to-equity ratio. Under these rules, if the average of a taxpayer's debt (with related and unrelated parties) exceeds the average amount of its equity for the respective fiscal year, the excess debt is treated as equity for income tax purposes. Consequently, the ability to deduct interests on related party loans may be affected.

I.3.3. CFC Legislation

The International Tax Transparency Regime provides that domiciled corporations or resident individuals who maintain and control investments, directly, indirectly, or through third parties in Low Tax Jurisdiction (LTJ) by means of branches, companies, real or movable property, shares, bank or investment accounts, trusts, temporary associations or any other kind of arrangement will be subject to the provisions of the International Tax Transparency Regime.

The terms stated herein will be applicable as long as the taxpayer is given the choice at the time the yields, profits or dividends derived from entities located in LTJ are distributed, or when said taxpayers control the administration of these entities, whether directly, indirectly or through a third party.

For such purposes, an investment is considered as located in a LTJ when one of the following circumstances is present:

- When accounts or investments are held with institutions located in said jurisdiction.
- When a domicile or post office address is available.
- When there is an effective headquarter.
- When there is a permanent establishment.
- When the investing party is incorporated or physically present in said jurisdiction.
- When any kind of legal business is carried out, regulated or perfected pursuant to the legislation of such jurisdiction.

Yields on investments held in a LTJ will be consider as taxable on an annual basis when generated, proportionally to the direct or indirect participation in said investment. This provision will be applicable even if the income, dividends or profits have not been distributed. Except for proof to the contrary, the amounts received in a LTJ will be considered (on an annual basis) as gross income or dividends derived from such investments.

As of today, the following countries are considered LTJ by Venezuela:

- Albania – Andorra – Angola
- Anguila – Antigua and Barbuda – Aruba
- Ascension – Bahamas – Bahrain
- Belize – Bermuda – British Virgin Islands
- Brunei – Campione D'Italia – Canary Special Zone
- Cape Verde – Cayman Islands – Channel Islands
- Christmas Island – Cocos Island – Cook Islands
- Cyprus – Djibouti – Dominica
- Dominican Republic – French Polynesia – Gabon
- Grenada – Greenland – Guam
- Guyana – Hong Kong – Honduras
- Isle of Man – Jordan – Kiribati
- Labuan – Lebanon – Liberia
- Liechtenstein – Luxemburg – Pacific Islands
- Puerto Rico – Saint Pierre and Miquelon – Macau
- Malta – Marshall Islands – Mauritius
- Monaco – Montserrat – Nauru
- Norfolk – Niue – Oman
- Ostrava Free Zone – Palau – Panama
- Pitcairn – Qeshm – Saint Helena
- Samoa – San Marino – Seychelles
- Solomon Islands – Sri Lanka – St Vincent and the Grenadines
- Svalbard – Swaziland – Tokelau
- Tristan da Cunha – Tunisia – Turks and Caicos
- Tuvalu – Uruguay – US Virgin Islands
- Vanuatu – Yemen

I.4. Tax Treaty Law

Treaties to Avoid Double Taxation (DTT) are conventions negotiated among countries, for the purposes of defining the fiscal treatment applicable to allow taxpayers have presence in both countries.

The ultimate goal of a DTT is to eliminate or reduce the impact that a double taxation may have on taxpayers, when there is attempt to levy the same income in both countries. This is achieve by allocating taxable matters between the countries. In addition to reducing or eliminating double taxation, DTTs also help to properly distribute fiscal income between the countries, prevent tax evasion, and promote the free flow of international trade.

With regards to hierarchy, in accordance with article 2 of the Venezuelan Master Tax Code, DTTs prevail over domestic income tax law. DTTs are standards of international legislation, and as such, they are to be construed according to the Vienna Convention regarding Treaties Legislation. These standards stipulate general principles relating good faith, the predominance of the text and the need to take into account the objective and purpose of the Treaty.

I.4.1. Adherence to UN or OECD MC

DTT´s entered into by Venezuela are mostly based on the model proposed by the Organization for Economic Cooperation and Development (OECD), published for the first time in 1963 and periodically reviewed ever since. These treaties reflect the consent of the Government on matters such as double taxation, source of income, taxpayers' identity, effective date, and administrative matters.

I.4.2. Special Features commonly present on Tax Treaties

There are no clauses that may differ from the OECD model.

I.4.3. Treaties Currently in Force

Venezuela has signed DTT's with the following countries:

Double tax treaties signed by Venezuela			
Austria	Barbados	Belarus	Belgium
Brazil	Canada	China	Cuba
Czech Republic	Denmark	France	Germany
Indonesia	Iran	Italy	Korea
Kuwait	Malaysia	Netherlands	Norway
Portugal	Qatar	Russia	Saudi Arabia
Spain	Sweden	Switzerland	Trinidad & Tobago
United Arab Emirates	United Kingdom	United States	Vietnam

I.5. Community Law

As mentioned before, Article 2 of the Venezuelan Master Tax Code provides that international treaties signed by Venezuela prevail over domestic income tax law.

I.5.1. Participation in a Community/Union

Venezuela is a member of the Mercosur trade agreement along with Argentina, Brazil, Paraguay and Uruguay (with Bolivia, Chile, Colombia, Ecuador and Peru as associate members). The agreement which sets out the basis for a common market among the member states aims to promote the free movement of goods, services and people by eliminating obstacles to regional trade. The trade of goods originating in, and proceeding from Mercosur countries is not subject to import duties, and a common external tariff applies for most of the tariff classification items.

Venezuela is also a member of the Latin America Integration Association (ALADI in Spanish), which includes all countries in South America and Mexico. ALADI aims to create a common market for the member countries through progressive tariffs reductions and to encourage free trade.

I.5.2. Rules regarding Corporate Income Taxation within the Community/Union

Neither Mercosur nor ALADI have enacted rules to regulate income tax or to mitigate double taxation among the member countries.

I.5.3. Jurisprudence regarding Corporate Income Taxation within the Community/Union

N/A

I.6. Influence of BEPS Action Plan on the Country

As of today, BEPS has not been considered in Venezuela.

I.6.1. Adoption of rules in line with BEPS Reports

No specific legislative changes have been made or proposed based on BEPS. Certain matters addressed by BEPS are already regulated by VITL and/or case law (substance requirements, thin capitalization rules, restrictions to interest deduction, among others).

I.6.2. Participation in Multilateral Instrument

None as of today. No commitment yet to introduce CbC reporting.

I.7. Jurisprudence

There has been no relevant tax case law in the past 5 years.